A New Paradigm

In this new series – **BIBLE THREADS, Keys to Understanding the Bible** – award-winning author Arlington McRae offers us a fresh new 21st century paradigm for how we approach the Bible and understand its essential message. Not a new message; but a new perspective of the Bible as a whole to significantly increase our understanding of it. This series is an invaluable resource to guide us on our journey to truly comprehending the Bible and its applicability to our lives.

The Bible For Beginners And the Rest of Us, the first volume in the series, offers us a power packed, Jesus inspired, potentially life-changing resource as it presents the Bible to us in its simplest form. Starting at the beginning, the author walks us through a new "perspective" and a new "context" for how we understand and interpret what we read. It is designed for (a) those of us new to the Bible, and (b) those who never received a comprehensive overview of the Bible that makes sense to them, that fills in the blanks. Additionally, in this volume, the author lays out the structure and the over all story – the big picture – of the Bible, to give us a broader context for how we interpret and unify the various books and stories.

Its purpose is to equip you to discover Bible truths for yourself. Therefore, at the completion of this volume, you will be encouraged to read your Bible and to study it more intelligently, with much more confidence, and with a satisfying sense of accomplishment.

From The Author

The Bible For Beginners And the Rest of Us is not just for beginners but also for those who never started at the beginning. What do I mean? Do you remember when you became a Christian? Did anyone guide you through the Bible story, in an orderly fashion, from the beginning to end? Do you have a systematic and logical understanding of the Bible's message? If not, this book is for you. Read it. Digest it. Then apply it as you read your Bible from cover to cover.

Remember to A.S.K. (Ask, Seek, Knock, Matthew 7:7-8) the Holy Spirit to teach you as you read. And please, do not forget to give Him thanks and praise daily for what He teaches you. And as always, all the glory belongs to God, the Father, and to His Son, Jesus!

This volume is published in two versions: <u>Standard</u> and <u>Expanded</u>. The Expanded Version includes the content of the Standard Version plus it adds an additional chapter and connects you to an extended library of relevant online resources to extend your biblical depth and comprehension.

May you enjoy it as much as I have.

Arlington McRae

THE
Bible For Beginners
And The Rest of Us

THE
Bible For Beginners

And The Rest of Us

A Guide to Making Basic Bible Sense

EXPANDED VERSION

Arlington McRae

Embassy One Publishers
Houston, Texas

Your comments about this book are encouraged and welcomed. Please post at Amazon.com's book review section and at the website below. Or, write to us at the email address. Thank you for your love.

This book is dedicated to my wife, Pauline, for her faithfulness to me and to Jesus Christ which she has affectionally demonstrated throughout our many years together by her steadfast love, patience, support and encouragement, and by sacrificing her time in order that I might have the freedom to complete my God-given assignments.

What was from the beginning, what we have heard, what we have seen with our eyes, what we beheld and our hands handled, concerning the Word of Life— 2and the life was manifested, and we have seen and bear witness and proclaim to you the eternal life, which was with the Father and was manifested to us— 3what we have seen and heard we proclaim to you also, that you also may have fellowship with us; and indeed our fellowship is with the Father, and with His Son Jesus Christ. 4And these things we write, so that our joy may be made complete. (1 John 1:1-4)

Contents

From The Series

BIBLE THREADS

Keys to Understanding the Bible

Volume I

Series Preface

Several years ago, I went to a national Christian bookstore chain just to browse. I stepped in, and immediately the Holy Spirit took charge and overwhelmed me with what at the time looked like thousands upon thousands of books that filled shelf after shelf after eight-foot shelf. Then He asked me, "Why all these books?" "Why?" I was silent. Then He said, "People spend much time reading books about the Bible; little time actually reading the Bible itself". But why? I pondered. Gradually sadness permeated my emotions. My heart was broken for I know the longings of the heart and the *urgent message* all peoples need to hear. I became even sadder because I understood their struggle.

There was a time, in my own life, when I would sit down to read the Bible; I would read ten to fifteen minutes and realize I had no idea or remembrance of what I had just read. I understood it as I was reading; but now, no recollection. I was an avid reader. I would read at least ten magazines per month from cover to cover and remember. But when I read the Bible, I was left with no understanding or penetration to my memory. What was the problem? Was this real? So I tested myself to see if I had lost my reading comprehension. I took out a magazine and read a paragraph. I had no problem. Then I took the Bible and read a paragraph. Nothing. It was as if I had not read one phrase. I wanted to read and understand the Bible. My parents raised me in church. I was a Christian. I had accepted Jesus as my Savior. Why could I not understand and retain what I was reading in the Bible? I finally figured out that the only thing that made some sense to me, that I could retain, were the words of Jesus. So I concentrated my reading on the red print of the New Testament. I have met other persons who say they have had similar experiences.

I realize my experience may be an extreme case. Perhaps you are not acquainted with what I experienced. But how many persons are there having trouble reading the Bible with understanding? We read book after book about the Bible but not the Bible itself. Perhaps you are one of those persons who is trying to read the Bible but you cannot make sense of it. Or it just doesn't seem to sink in. Why is that? Yes, "The god of this world has blinded the minds of the unbelieving, that they might not see the light of the gospel of the glory of Christ" (2 Corinthians 4:4). But what about the many believers? Why don't we understand the Bible in a truly life-changing way? I am convinced it is primarily because we lack the keys to unlock its powerful, life-changing message.

This series is designed to present you the keys as a kick-start to propel you to higher heights in God through greater understanding of the Bible – His revelation of Himself and of all mankind.

Series Introduction

In the mid 1990's, God spoke audibly to me and instructed me saying, "Feed My sheep". After a couple of weeks of pondering what God had spoken, I accepted His appointment to ministry. I began to enhance my biblical knowledge by taking courses offered by my church. Upon completion of those courses, I enrolled in a Bible college and completed seventeen credit hours. God again spoke audibly to me and instructed me to go to a specific seminary and get a master's degree, which I completed in December 2006.

In September 2000, while in seminary, I suffered what has been called a massive heart attack. During that heart attack, I died. The medics worked extremely hard for a long time to bring me back to life. When they brought me back, I remained in a coma for three days. All my major organs were losing their function as I lay in a coma and afterwards. Doctors told my wife, Pauline, to expect the worst. But her faith in Jesus, the Christ, saw a different outcome. She believed in her heart of hearts that God loved her husband as I had told her so many times in the past. In spite of the doctors' hopeless prognosis, she was convinced I would recover. In the hospital, the nursing staff called me "the miracle man".

During the onset of the heart attack, God came to visit me in my home. Unlike any other experience with God in the past, God's all-encompassing presence came to my house to visit me! His presence filled the room. It permeated my whole being. I can tell you with certainty that when you are saturated with the presence of the Almighty, loving God, when you are one with Him, the only thing that matters is God. That experience and the grace of God, along with much prayer and supplications, has given me a much deeper appreciation for the reality and the person of God.

Whatever He Wants

God, our heavenly Father, has shown me that most of us have our lives filled with so much "clutter" we do not have time for His presence. We are running around here "busy as a beaver". When we can, we allocate a little time to fit God into our busy schedules. A life of "clutter" ought not be our normal. When the presence of the living God has fully engulfed you, you do not worry about fitting anything in but God. You do not want anything else but God. My prayer is that you too will come to experience God's presence, and His all-encompassing love, as I have. That is likely to happen only when He is the foremost priority in your life.

I have told you all these things as a backdrop to tell you this. Because of the heart attack experience, I examined my life before the heart attack. I am two months beyond the heart attack now and I am looking at my life. I am talking with God; spending all my time with Him. I really could not do much else because I am very weak. I am recuperating very slowly with the aid of my wife, Pauline. I am learning that up until about three years before the heart attack, I did what I wanted to do with my life. Oh, I had a little God time here and there. I was doing some of the things that God wanted me to do. I went to church on Sunday. I was on the trustee board of my church and in the men's choir. I even led a couple of songs. But other than Sunday and a few meetings from time to time during the week, I did what I wanted to do with my life. Primarily, I lived my life my way, not God's way. I was *self-focused* rather than being *God-focused*. What I came to realize from the heart attack experience is that God is the One Who came running after me to bring me back to life.

The only reason I live today is because God did not want me dead. He wanted me alive for Him, for His purpose (Reference 1 Peter 4:1-3). That is what He always had in mind for me. But I wasted much of my past. When He pursued me, I did not listen. Not intentionally, but I ignored His soft tender voice and His frequent urges too many times because I had not been instructed on hearing his voice, on knowing His beckoning call (Reference 1 Samuel 3:1-9). Therefore, following the heart attack, I committed to Jesus that I would live the rest of my new life for Him, for His purpose. I would give up what I want. Whatever He wants, that is what I want. Therefore, as I write these words, that is my motivation, to do what God wants done, and hopefully, to help you move to that same place where you will want to do with your life only what God wants done; and to encourage you to seek an intimate relationship with Him where you will want to spend hours each day with Him instead of electronic gadgets and television. It can be done; and you can do it!

They Are Only Toys

What is your idea of success? What is your vision of the good life? Not too long ago, I thought success was having large bank accounts, fine cars in my driveway, and a huge house. To be frank, these things are great to have. Viewed appropriately, they can greatly enhance one's life. But God has shown me that there is a higher life.

One of the things God has taught me is a new perspective on the world's "things" from iPods to giant skyscrapers. He told me they have no value. They are "vanity". "How can that be, God, when we place so much value in them, from a few dollars to millions?" "If they have no value, then, what are they?" He said, "Toys". Now I am bewildered. After much prayer and meditation, I have come to appreciate God's perspective.

Children love their toys. They are extremely possessive when it comes to their toys. They will even hurt another child, severely, for their toys. We are just like our children and grandchildren with their toys. We adults love our toys – cars, houses, smart phones, iPads, iPods, tablets, flat screen TV's, electronic gadgets, sports, money, buildings, etc., etc. And we will hurt someone, even kill, because of our toys. But all these toys that Satan has built up to look and feel so good, are being used to keep us from spending time with our God and Father. We are not the only generation to have this problem.

The Israelites had this problem when they settled in the land of Canaan, "a land flowing with milk and honey"; containing houses they did not build and vineyards they did not plant. When they prospered, they turned more and more to their "things" and away from their God. In time, they became envious of their neighbors who had gods they could see. That was Satan's big play, to create envy in them for vain things. He has not changed. And why should he? His play works so well. Therefore, today, we must be aware, at all times, that Satan is working diligently to divert our attention away from our God and Father, and from our Savior and Lord, Jesus, the Christ. And for what reason does he do this? You do know that God desires all your time? He is a jealous God. He loves spending time with you. Therefore, Scripture has commanded us to "pray without ceasing", i.e., converse with Him. Satan's goal is to derail or prevent any such relationship from ever forming.

God Wants To Be In Your Life

Prayer is talking to God and interacting with Him in a two-way conversation. In case you do not know it, let me state it emphatically, **God loves you!!** Yes. You! And He really wants you to spend all your time with Him. I like to think of it this way. Scripture says, "pray without ceasing". And I used to wrestle with that concept. I have other things I must do. How can I pray without ceasing? How can I spend all my time conversing with God? How can I pray all the time? Well I tell you, I look at it like this. Let's say the two of us are enjoying one another's company, and having a wonderful conversation on a long leisurely walk in the country. We are walking and talking and we run into someone else. So we might stop and spend some time talking to that other person. After we have talked to that other person for a while, we would continue our walking and talking. As we are walking, something else catches my attention some distance out. I begin to focus on that thing that is out there in the distance. Because my attention is diverted, you may not say anything to me for a while. And I may not say anything to you. As we continue walking, we start talking again, perhaps about my distraction or on a brand new subject, maybe on some of my innermost thoughts. As our trip continues, other matters and events may punctuate our conversation. Well, you can see in this example that it really was an unceasing conversation with each other broken up by events here and there like when the third person came in and we dealt with that interruption. But basically, we communicated all during the trip. That is the position God wants in our day-to-day lives. He wants us to include Him, to walk and talk with Him.

He knows we have other things to do. But He really would like to be involved in everything we do. If He is, He can smooth out the rough places and the steep hills in our lives. Like your sitting here reading this book, you could invite God's participation. You could say to God, "Lord, this man, I hope he has something to tell me that is worth hearing. Open my mind to hear him. Open my heart to receive his message" And when I have said something that doesn't quite make good sense, you might say, "God, I do not understand what he is talking about. Please, Lord, help me to see it clearly?" Please take me seriously because the devil does his job very well. You may receive what I am saying initially, but the devil is going to try to make sure you do not remember it or value it after today or in a week, or maybe in a month. Or, he may distort it to confuse you to keep you from seeing the true picture. So get God involved in helping you to understand, accept, value, and remember what you read from this point on. Learn to "pray without ceasing" (1 Thessalonians 5:16-18). Even if you are not a believer, pray anyway. Begin by asking Him to make you a believer. What harm can it do?

He Deserves Our Best

God's business deserves our very best effort. Therefore, I encourage you to study diligently and make notes. And make sufficient notes so you can go back and read them again and again, to absorb fully the concepts we are presenting so you can then teach others. That is a primary characteristic of a true disciple, as well as one who is seeking God but has yet to find Him. As you teach, do not teach solely from what your memory says but from your copious notes. You may not realize it but repetition is the best learning method for the human mind. I can say that without fear of contradiction. So you say, "How can you be so confident" Because my Father in heaven uses that same method in His Bible. If He thinks I need repetition, then I know I need it. How does He use the same method? Look at your Bible. It contains a lot of repetition. The message of the Bible is simple. But He keeps telling it to us over and over. From different perspectives, He goes a little deeper, and a little wider, to help us grasp the broader message of the central story. But it's the same message over and over again. So, by writing it, reviewing it, and meditating on it, the message is reinforced in your memory and eventually it penetrates to your heart. From there, it is manifested in your thought process, and in the way you live your life as a disciple, witness, and teacher for Jesus, the Christ.

Let me give you another reason why I am asking you to make

notes. Some of us have bad memories. So what we hear today we may not remember half of it by tomorrow or in a week. I am not asking you to re-write this book series. But I am asking you to make copious notes on those items that speak to your heart and/or to your spirit. Definitely document what your spirit hears from God, exactly as you hear it. Add your editorial comments to it if you must. But first write exactly what God speaks to your spirit. When we write it down, that will help us to remember. Second, if we need to go back to refresh our recollection, we have precise documentation to do that. Third, if we want to share our thoughts and insights with others, we have an exact rendering of them written at the time we received them. This is important! Very important!

During my first couple of years in college, my professors regularly stressed the point that, "if you are not writing, you are not studying". Therefore, let me give you this perspective on notes. The Bible teaches us that, as Christians, we are all priests for the Most High God. The Israelites, the entire nation, were priests for the Most High God. They were to become more like God and less like the society around them. They were to live the life that God laid out for them. By their example, they were to be teachers for God. Their lives, their culture, and their testimonies were to teach others about their Creator. God has put that same responsibility on those of us who are Christians (1 Peter 2:9-12). Therefore, I strongly recommend that you obtain a spiral notebook (perhaps two) with sufficient pages for maintaining all your thoughts, questions, answers, and notes on what you learn throughout the rest of our sessions together. A spiral notebook is bound securely so you do not lose sheets, thereby making it excellent for maintaining permanent notes. Or, consider making digitized notes on your laptop, tablet or smart phone. If you digitize your notes, be sure to make frequent redundant backups that you keep in multiple, very safe, places. This too, is extremely important.

You will obtain far more return from the investment of your time and money if you commit yourself to making notes as the Holy Spirit gives you insight with understanding. Your notes could very well transform your own life or the lives of your family members, friends, neighbors and co-workers. So please, make copious notes and share them. Else, the devil may snatch your newly acquired biblical understanding and perspective from you thereby reducing your effectiveness and your eternal rewards in the everlasting kingdom of Jesus Christ.

A final comment on notes – hold on to your unresolved issues. As you journey deeper into the series, let's see if you and I can come to some kind of reasonable accommodation for each of us by the time you complete the first two books in this series; certainly by the time you reach the end of this series. You may have questions anywhere along the way. So write them down and look for the answers as you read. The series will not answer all your questions. It is meant only as a guide to aid your Bible study. Hopefully, it will put you on a path to discovering answers for yourself. And when your questions are answered, at a minimum, make a note of the answer along with an indication of the location – volume and page number, or Internet article title or URL – where the answer is found. Keep your notes well organized and leave sufficient space on each issue for future additions. Pre-plan the structure of your notes. Organize your notes well so you can locate your answers at will as you meditate on the biblical concepts and as you share your new insights with family, friends, neighbors, and co-workers. May God reward your diligence by sending others to you for you to educate and provide answers to their questions.

A primary objective of this series is for us to get all its concepts etched into our brains, and eventually into our hearts through repetition and meditation. Then incorporate them into our daily Bible study, from which we learn the way we should live our lives for Jesus Christ. So, give Him your very best and He will reward you accordingly.

Bible Threads

I grew up on a farm in North Carolina. From time to time, we would have quilting parties. Neighbors would come to our home to help us make quilts. I enjoyed these times playing with their children and helping with the quilting. I especially enjoyed the quilting. A quilt is made using multiple layers of materials that are sown together to hold the layers in place. One of the things I would do is thread my needle with as long a line of thread as I could handle. I was attempting to use a single piece of thread from one end of the quilt to the other. Often I would stitch a design in the quilt as I worked. But more times than I can count, my thread ran out long before I reached the other end. So I would tie another very long thread to the first one in such a way that one could not see the knot. To the casual eye, the stitch looked like one continuous thread. We made our quilts from multi-colored scraps of cloth my mother would save from her sewing projects. Sometimes, I would use colored thread that matched the dominant patches of cloth in the quilt. Therefore, one would notice that at times, the contrasting threads would be quite visible. But in other patches, the thread would barely be noticed because the thread and the patches were so similar in color. God has done the same thing in His Bible.

God has woven overarching unifying themes (i.e., threads) into the pages of the biblical text to unify (keep together, hold together, or link together) the various narratives and stories, which on the surface, may seem to have nothing in common with one another. Alternatively, one could say that God has wrapped the narratives and stories around overarching themes or threads. The biblical authors have written from the perspective that the reader already knows these threads. Sometimes these threads are conspicuous and obvious. At other times, the reader must search for them. Identify these threads and you have the keys to interpreting and understanding the characters, their acts, and their motivation from God's perspective. These threads not only provide God's perspective but they also illumine the broader context for everything written in the biblical text. Look for and observe these threads as you study, and the Bible will begin to make perfectly good sense to you.

Keys To Understanding The Bible

One intent of this series – BIBLE THREADS: Keys To Understanding The Bible – is to provide not only new and significant information simply and clearly, but also to be motivational and life changing for both believers and non-believers as you learn to study the Bible more intelligently. My prayer is that you will not only read all the books in this series but also diligently study them, and the referenced Internet articles. Then use what you have learned to read and study your Bible, enlisting the aid of the Holy Spirit, Who will teach us if we ask. Scripture, speaking of the things important to God, encourages you to "Ask, and it shall be given to you; seek, and you shall find; knock, and it shall be opened to you" (Matthew 7:7-8). Then, take what you receive, no matter how little or how great, and teach others. Your efforts are sure to yield great rewards not only for your own life here on earth and in eternity, but also for the lives of all those you touch. Keep in mind that, today, you have the ability, from your home, to touch lives all over the worlds via the Internet.

At this writing, my goal is to provide the primary keys (i.e., threads) to understanding the Bible in four volumes:

Volume I – *The Bible for Beginners And The Rest of Us: A Guide to Making Basic Bible Sense* – introduces you to the Bible and provides an eagle-eye view of the Bible and its essential message. I have attempted to provide significant information in a compact volume that is brief and to the point. A major part of its core content is contained in chart form with the understanding that "a picture is worth a thousand words". In addition to the text, expanded discussion and/or additional content by other more reputable authors is available in the Expanded Version via insightful Internet articles easily accessible on the BibleThreads.net website (or via live web links in the digital versions).

Volume II – *Born Dead* – presents the dominant thread for

understanding the Bible. Its design is to present a biblical perspective of God and man through God's eyes, and to provide a Bible centered context for the church – "the called out ones".

Volume III – *A Hostile Environment: A World of Lies, Conflict, and Deception* – presents an enlightened picture of the hostility (the enmity) in the world between the "seed" of the serpent and the "seed" of the woman by exploring its cause and the resulting turmoil and violence from Genesis through Revelation, to include even the present day.

Volume IV – *The Bible in 3D* – argues that, while the primary focus of the Bible in this present age is making "disciples of all the nations", the program of God also includes "the rulers and the authorities in the heavenly places".

Throughout this series, you will encounter references and bridges to valuable resources by other faithful servants of God. At the outset, I determined not to rewrite what other servants have spent years developing. That would not be a good use of my time and gifts. This approach allows me to stay in the big picture, or at the summary level and let others provide the details. Combined, our resources should provide sufficient coverage of the Bible to satisfy your quest to know the person of God, the Bible's message and its importance to your life.

Bible Believing Jesus Disciples

The stated goal of my seminary degree program was to teach us how to study the Bible. My goal in this series is not to teach you how to study the Bible. There are many well-written resources for that. Rather, my goal is to provide you the keys to unlock its treasure chest. If I do my job well, you will be able to extract and understand the Bible's essential message in a way that will allow you to accept it and live it; then, teach others who in turn will do the same. My prayer is that this will become an unbroken chain eventually touching the lives of 100's of millions of lost souls all around the globe. I invite you to join others who are already active participants in this process. Begin by starting your own link in this chain by gathering study partners and by regularly sharing this book series with as many people as you can. Give it as birthday and Christmas gifts. Inspire and implore them to commit to reading and meditating on the Bible daily.

The ultimate goal of this series is to create a worldwide host of Bible believing Jesus disciples by providing you the enlightenment, the encouragement, and the enthusiasm to joyfully read and diligently study the Bible, each and every day, with deep understanding and with *insight* – your ability to accurately perceive and clearly articulate its illuminating truth. Then allow the Bible to dictate how you prioritize and live your life. Come join us on this exciting journey!

When you have completed your study of each book in this series, and when you have completed this entire series, perhaps a systematic review of its concepts, assertions, and implications for your life and the lives of your family, friends, neighbors, and associates might be in order.

PRAYER: May Jesus, the Christ, God's Messiah, reward your reading, study efforts, meditations, and ruminations with great insight and deep understanding beyond your wildest expectations. I pray that one outcome of your reading and study efforts is that you come to know Jesus intimately and that you experience the blessed life of Deuteronomy 30 "by loving the Lord your God, by obeying His voice, and by holding fast [clinging] to Him; for this is your life and the length of your days" (v 20). This we ask in Jesus name. Amen!

THE
Bible For Beginners

And The Rest of Us

A Guide to Making Basic Bible Sense

Expanded Version

Arlington McRae

Volume Preface

Whether you are seeking God or you are a committed unbeliever, you want to know if there truly is a god. If there is, what you have learned about Him thus far is sporadic, piecemeal, and inconsistent, having too many gaps, lacking coherency – i.e., a logical, orderly, and consistent relationship of its parts. You think knowledge of God should be completely logical and His ways understandable. You want to know if the Bible can be trusted. But for you, there are too many unanswered questions. I understand your frustration. I lived it. But today, I am at peace. God, my heavenly Father, has taught me all I need to know to experience peace in my quest to know Him and to have more of Him. And I believe the reason you are holding this book is because the God of the Bible loves you and wants an intimate relationship with you too.

If you are a Christian (or maybe one raised in the church but have yet to truly submit and commit to Jesus Christ), you may be struggling as well to find coherency in the Bible. "Law, history, Gospels, Psalms: how do these divisions relate one to another?" "What is the simple message of the Bible?" "What is God's will for my life?" These are all legitimate questions. Sunday after

Sunday, we may listen to sermon after sermon with no apparent relationship to one another and little relationship to how we actually live our lives. Far too many of us struggle to relate Sunday activities to the rest of the week. We know God is out there somewhere. At least we hope He is. "But when is He going to intervene in my struggles, in my lack, in my emptiness?" With greater understanding of Him, and who we are as human beings, we would come to realize that He already has intervened in so many wonderful ways. And we would find our security and significance in Him rather than broken relationships, and "things" of the world.

The unbeliever and the Christian struggle alike because we lack the light of an illuminating "perspective" and "context" (a new twenty-first century paradigm) from which we can make sense of God's Word, discover solid biblical truths, and learn how to apply them to the way we actually live our lives (Christianity is a new way of life, not a religion). Still, the God of the Bible is wooing us because He truly loves us – unbelievers and Christians – and He is seeking an intimate love relationship with each of us. We would come to know and appreciate that if only we could learn to read the Bible with genuine understanding.

Or, perhaps you are searching for the purpose of life? Perhaps you lack motivation, optimism, or contentment. Perhaps your life lacks meaning. Your big question might well be, "Why are we here?" To you I say, learn of Jesus, the Son of God. He is what you are missing. He is what you are actually seeking.

The answers we are all seeking, to the questions that truly matter, are in the Bible and in God's Son, Jesus. This volume, and those which follow, is my attempt to encourage you, to guide you and to help you to begin your own journey to truly understanding and appreciating the significance of the entire Bible – the authentic revelation of the only true and living God.

The purpose of this book,
indeed, this entire series,
is to provide a biblical

Perspective & Context

to help you read and
understand the Bible,
the revelation of
the only true and living God.

How To Use This Volume

When studied carefully, this book will point you in the direction to finding the best that Jesus has to offer. It is not offered simply to tell you what I say. Instead, it is designed to help you discover for yourself and understand what God says. It presents a process, not a one-time reading event. It is a small volume, but it is packed with vital knowledge. So apply it every time you study the Scriptures. We are certain you will come to value its content more and more as you do. We pray and it is our hope that the results will bring you much joy.

You might think of this book as providing three levels of knowledge with each one building on the other. The three levels include, (a) the written text including quotations, (b) the referenced Scriptures in the appendix, and (c) the referenced web articles.

Think of this book also as Jesus' outstretched hand in darkness beckoning you to come closer to Him. You can hear His voice. But all you can see is darkness. Therefore, you must grope about for Him. That is the effort you must make to lay hold of His person. I have already made the effort (through twenty years of intense Bible study) to make this book as easy as possible for you to follow and grasp. We even fixed it so you don't even need to purchase a Bible. All you have to do is make a few steps of your own and have an Internet connection.

Speaking of steps, I believe most God seekers and students of the Word of God will achieve maximum benefit from the whole of their investment in this book by approaching it in three phases, according to the three levels of knowledge incorporated herein:

First, quickly read the book from cover to cover to include the charts and only quoted Scriptures; pausing frequently to ponder and visualize a picture of what you have read and how it might apply to you. Also take this time to make written notes. Skip the referenced (underlined) Scriptures and referenced web articles (i.e., the underlined article titles) as well as the Scripture references included in the charts. We expect you will find this first pass a quick read. No Bible is required. This first pass may prove sufficient for many seasoned Bible students.

Second, along with a study partner (recommended), reach deeper by reading the book again more slowly and more thoughtfully. Meditate on, and consider seriously each significant point. Take the time to ponder and explore each and every significant point –.e.g., what does it say and how does it impact your thinking? This time, using the included underlined Scripture references (Scriptures are located in the Appendix) or if you desire, your own Bible, or an online Bible study tool such as www.biblegateway.com or https://net.bible.org, incorporate the text of all the referenced Scriptures in your study (including those in the charts). Pause to ponder their meaning and significance to the point this book is making. Ask yourself, "What does this Scripture passage add to the author's point?" Again, skip the referenced web articles.

Third, for those who desire to reach even deeper into God's Word, do a cursory read of this book a third time but make careful study of each referenced web article (scan QR code to access the online list of articles at biblethreads.net or enter the URL). Using each article's internal hyperlinks (if available), your Bible or an online Bible study tool such as www.biblegateway.com or https://net.bible.org, incorporate the article's referenced Scriptures into your study. This time, multiple study partners would be especially beneficial in helping you explore the deep recesses of God's word.

QR Code

Along the way, use what you have learned to practice applying your new knowledge to your Bible study. When you have finished this volume, make it a habit to apply all you have learned to enjoy your study and examination of God's Word. It truly is food for the soul (Matthew 4:1-4).

When this book asks, "Any questions?" that is your queue to make notes to yourself including listing on paper or in a computer, any questions in your mind at that point. As you proceed through this book, look for answers to your questions. Also look for further explanations or insights into what you already know or have recently learned. Take time to enjoy the process!

Each time you and your study partners sit down to read this book, and to read and study the Bible, you will find it extremely beneficial to remember to pause, and seek God's assistance through prayer. Whether you are a believer or not, take time to pray! Ask Him especially to guide you and to teach you what He wants you to learn today. Then follow your spirit's lead. God may point you to various Scriptures that may appear to be disconnected. Follow His lead. And please be confident in knowing that He is faithful and trustworthy to answer that prayer because He has made a promise to do so (Matthew 7:7-8).

Part 1

Perspective

*There was the true Light [Jesus] which, coming
into the world, enlightens every man. He was in
the world, and the world was made through Him,
and the world did not know Him. He came to His
own [Israel], and those who were His own did not
receive Him. But as many as received Him, to
them He gave the right to become children of
God, even those who believed in His name.*
John 1:9-12

1

Seeking God's Perspective

Typically, in church, we drop new Christians into our instructional programs like dropping a boatload of lost souls in the middle of the ocean. No matter which way they look, all they see is water. No matter which direction they choose to go, the outcome is the same – hopelessness. They will still be lost until they can see the shoreline in the far distance. In the same way, we drop new believers into the vast ocean of God's Word. Week after week, year after year, we feed them small bits and pieces of the whole of God's Word. They attempt to sort and store the pieces in a logical pattern so they make sense. They are striving to visualize a unified efficacious message from the whole of God's Word. But try as they might, their efforts seem useless. Therefore, in time, too many give up trying and become imitators. If the Word of God is to be logical and aesthetically consistent for unbelievers and for new believers, if they are to have a solidly biblical perspective for assimilating and integrating biblical content, we must start them at the beginning. Then follow a logical and consistent pattern that leads to an understanding of a coherent whole. Moreover, we must do the same for seasoned Christians who have yet to acquire an insightful coherent whole of God's Word from God's perspective.

The Learning Process

God designed the human brain to observe, feel, listen, read, accumulate, record, organize, assimilate, correlate, and retrieve information in a logical and consistent manner. From infancy, we are collecting and recording bits and pieces of information. At first, we accumulate many pieces of data looking for a connection between them. If no connection is found, that piece of data is stored in its own brain-folder. We attempt to connect and store each new piece of information with data already organized and stored in the various folders of our brain. When we have collected sufficient data in a folder on a given subject, concept, or thing, we attempt to organize it in a manner that yields coherency within that subject area, and to connect it with any other bits of data stored in other folders. If we are successful, having sufficient data on a given subject, we are able to discover logic, order, and aesthetic consistency. Therefore, we are able to draw valid conclusions from a given subject and determine its relationship to other subjects.

Baby Christians begin life in much the same way as natural babies. Void of sufficient Bible knowledge, they observe, feel, listen, read, accumulate, record, organize, and attempt to assimilate, correlate, and retrieve biblical information in a logical

48

and consistent manner. This should enable them to draw logical, consistent, and valid conclusions and to develop their own sense of perspective from which to analyze and evaluate all future input and actions. Unfortunately, for far too many of us – unbelievers, beginners and mature Christians – it has not worked out the way God intended.

This book, and this entire series, is my attempt to introduce you to the Bible in a manner that will enable you to read your Bible and draw logical and consistently valid conclusions. Prayerfully, this will lead you to a God illuminated perspective for reading, scrutinizing, and understanding the Bible, God's revelation of Himself to us, and particularly, God's revelation of Himself to you. Only then will you come to know the true meaning of who God is, who man is and who you are; and thereby begin to appreciate the mighty and magnificent work Jesus Christ has already performed on your behalf. From this foundation, new and experienced believers can begin to understand and value the program of God and their role in it; and thereby, be motivated to commit themselves totally to Jesus Christ and His ministry of reconciliation (2 Corinthians 5:14-21).

Perspective

We have difficulty with our biblical perspective because we usually learn the Bible piecemeal. From childhood or as mature adults, we are bombarded with disconnected messages from the Bible. Even our own reading tends to be sporadic and disconnected. Therefore, we are inclined to see the Bible as bits and pieces of good information and wise sayings. This way of viewing the Bible becomes so engraved in our minds that we strongly resist any effort to change it. How and what we learn first tends to influence how and what we will learn thereafter. Our method of viewing the Bible and studying it is rooted typically in tradition. Some treat the Bible as a wonderful book of wise and famous sayings without knowing its power. Some read the Bible because they saw mom or granny reading it or because the pastor encouraged them to. Oftentimes, Sunday school and Bible study offer little to improve on this picture.

When I conversed with God about how I might truly understand the Bible, He said, "*Perspective* and *Context*". Here we address the concept of *perspective*. We shall discuss *context* beginning in chapter 4.

Over the last several years, God has been teaching me what He means by perspective and context. My simple definition for perspective is, "a way of perceiving or looking at something, the lens or viewpoint through which one perceives an idea, a person, place, or thing". According to the experts, and the definition we shall use for our discussion, *perspective* is, "The ability to perceive things in their actual interrelations or comparative importance", "the proper or accurate point of view", "one's mental view of facts, ideas, etc., and their interrelationships", "the ability to see all the relevant data in a meaningful relationship" (Reference thefreedictionary.com).

A God Perspective Versus Tradition

Have you ever asked God to help you see the Bible through His eyes? I strongly recommend it each time you study your Bible.

Typically, we read the Bible from the traditional perspective. That is, from man as the starting point looking outward to God. For far too many of us, we want to know how to get God's assistance in our plans, how to get Him to give us what we want. That is why we think bumper stickers like "God Is My Co-pilot" are great because we want to be in charge. Our focus is always me, me, and me too. In typical conversation, we often overwork the words "I", "me", and "my". Pay attention to your own words sometimes. We want to know, "What has God done for me lately?" However, the Bible reveals that God made us; and He made us for His purpose, not the other way around.

The Bible actually begins with God, not man. A proper biblical *perspective*, then, starts with God, and looking outward through God's eyes to see mankind (and the earth) as God sees them. From God's perspective, we can observe and appreciate God's heart, His actions and reactions in light of the truth of man. For example, when we look around at mankind, we see beautiful "*life*". However, when God looks at man, He sees "*death*" and "*darkness*". There is another dimension to life and knowledge – a spiritual dimension. "'For My thoughts are not your thoughts, Neither are your ways My ways', declares the Lord. 'For as the heavens are higher than the earth, So are My ways higher than your ways, And My thoughts than your thoughts', says the Lord". (Isaiah 55:8-9).

Now, let's see what God has to teach us about *Perspective*.

2

Beginning At The Beginning

Are you good at telling stories? Have you ever attempted to tell a friend about an incident or situation you experienced without starting at the very beginning? Usually what happens in those cases, your friend tends to interrupt you many times. Therefore, when you finally reach the punch line, they will not even hear it because what they hear will not make sense until they hear all its details from the beginning. You know the story very well. So you might not realize that you have skipped over crucial pieces of information. The pieces may be insignificant to you. But the story has to make sense to them. I don't know about you, but I have had that experience on many occasions, on both ends of the conversation. And it has taught me to be concerned about my listener and attentive to their perception of what I am saying. Starting at the very beginning is not always necessary. But often times, it is critical for clear communication even though the listener is familiar with the subject matter.

Now, I realize you might know the following information already. But in our journey, we're going to start close enough to the beginning so that those who know absolutely nothing can achieve sufficient comprehension so that the chapters to follow will be clear. Our beginning starts with the Bible and its structure.

The Bible contains sixty-six books divided into two major divisions – Old Testament and New Testament, or Old Covenant and New Covenant. Each of these is further divided into subdivisions. Most Bibles do not include the subdivisions in their table of contents. For a breakdown of the testaments into their subdivisions and books, see the chart, The Bible is a Library by the First Parish United Church of Christ. Each book contains numbered chapters and verses. For example, the book of Matthew, the first book of the New Testament, contains 28 chapters. Chapter 28 contains 20 verses. Chapter and verse numbers were created sometime around the thirteenth century AD to make it easy to reference and locate a particular portion of the Scriptures. The reference format specifies the book name, chapter and verse. A colon is used to separate chapter and verse. For example, the passage of Scriptures known as the Great Commission is found in Matthew chapter 28, verses 16 through 20. The format for its reference location is therefore, "Matthew 28:16-20". Oftentimes, the book names are abbreviated in the reference such as, "Mat 28:16-20". Most Bibles provide a table of abbreviated names in their front matter.

Bible Divisions

For this section, we shall address the included chart titled "Bible

Divisions" (end of chapter). Please take a moment now to review the chart. OK. Good. Welcome back.

First, this chart was created from a mental picture that God had given me. I did not know I had software that could make such a diagram. So I just happened to open my software and begin to work with it. Lo and behold, I was able to produce a chart that looks exactly like the picture God gave me.

So let's make a quick survey of our chart. The Bible is divided into two major divisions – Old Testament and New Testament or the Old and New Covenants. The Old Testament is composed of the circle immediately below Deuteronomy and all that is above that circle. The bottom circle depicts the New Testament. Now, what are some of the things that God wants us to see in this chart?

The Old Testament

If you will, notice, at the top is the *Pentateuch.* The Pentateuch, otherwise known as the Law of Moses or the Torah, designates the first five books of the Bible – Genesis through Deuteronomy. Now, you will observe that we have the Pentateuch and we have Deuteronomy there at the bottom of the Pentateuch. Together these make up the entirety of the Pentateuch. Here is the point that the chart is making in regard to the Pentateuch as a whole and Deuteronomy in particular. Everything before Deuteronomy is pointing to (leading up to) Deuteronomy. In other words, Genesis through Numbers is pointing to Deuteronomy. Deuteronomy restates and emphasizes the salient provisions of God's covenant with the Israelites – the first four books. To put it more precisely,

Deuteronomy presents and defines the type of relationship God insists on having with His chosen people. That is why I call Deuteronomy the *"Book of Relationship"*.

For an understanding of the nature and content of the Pentateuch, see the article, The Law: The First Five Books by J. Hampton Keathley III.

Below Deuteronomy, we have the next level depicting the rest of the Old Testament divided into the *History* books, the *Prophets*, and *Wisdom and Poetry*.

History takes us from the book of Joshua through the books of Nehemiah and Esther. Nehemiah is the end of the Old Testament history for the nation of Israel. The events in Esther occurred during the period covered by Ezra. For a survey of these books, see the article, The Historical Books by J. Hampton Keathley III.

The kings of Israel – before and after the kingdom was divided into the northern kingdom (Israel) and the southern kingdom (Judah) – take up a large portion of the historical period. The Bible presents the kings in the books of Samuel, Kings, and Chronicles. For a summary perspective of the Bible's emphasis for the period of the kings, see Israel, History Of, 2, IV. The Kingdom: Israel-Judah and other links at the top of the page.

See the chart, The Kings of Israel and Judah by Alan S.L. Wong that reveals the nature of each king's heart in relationship to God's covenant. The king was supposed to be God's mediator between Him and His people. Instead of obedience to the dictates of the covenant, most did evil in the eyes of the Lord. This chart provides links to a summary biography of each king and links to Scriptures addressing how the king ruled over God's people.

For a detail chart of the kings with Scripture references and extensive links to published commentary and Scriptures on each king and the prophet(s) of his day, see the Bible Reference Guide's chart, Kings of Israel and Judah.

In the Chart of Israel's and Judah's Kings and Prophets by Craig T. Owens, the author not only delineates how the king's behavior (relative to the covenant) looked to God, but he also presents the prophets who served God during the king's reign. This chart allows the Bible student to correlate the Scriptures relating to the king with the Scriptures relating to the prophet who served God during the king's reign.

The succeeding subdivision in our chart is the Prophets – Major & Minor. God employed prophets to deliver His message to the people. The books of the prophets can be placed in a linear chronology chart directly under the history books. In other words, the events in the prophets occurred at the same time as those in the history books. The prophets present a dramatic portrayal of man through the eyes of God's heart. Therefore, the prophets provide insight into the person and heart of God. From one perspective, we see Him as Father, disappointed and heartbroken, a strict disciplinarian to His terribly disobedient children. On the other hand, we see Him as the loving and compassionate Father; gracious even to His ruthless, selfish, unloving, evil children, to whom He promises a future and a hope with immeasurable blessings. To the nations surrounding Israel, He is the God to be feared and respected. The prophet's message could be revelations, instructions and guidance, or predictions of future events, good or bad. But more often than not, time after time, God's message was a serious complaint accompanied by what He intended to do about Israel's covenant violations should the people persist in their wrong doing (e.g., Jeremiah 11:1-11). Some prophets served God at the same time as others. The prophets begin with the book of Isaiah and end with Malachi. They are presented, not in chronological order, but primarily by the size of the book.

The Major Prophets, the larger books, are Isaiah, Jeremiah, Lamentations (authored by Jeremiah), Ezekiel, and Daniel. See the article, The Major Prophets by J. Hampton Keathley III for a survey of these prophets.

From Hosea to Malachi are the Minor Prophets, i.e., the short books. However, the size of the book is no indication of the significance of its message. See the article The Minor Prophets by J. Hampton Keathley III for a survey of the Minor Prophets.

The prophets may be further divided into those appointed to the northern kingdom of Israel versus those appointed to the southern kingdom of Judah. Additionally, the prophets are categorized according to their appearance before, during, and after Judah's exile to Babylon – i.e., pre-exilic, exilic, and post-exilic prophets, respectively.

For a thoughtful perspective of the prophets, study the article, Understanding the Writing Prophets by Jim Ellis.

Our next subdivision – Wisdom & Poetry – is positioned in the Bible immediately after the history books and before the prophets. These books share wisdom (e.g., Proverbs), worship

(Psalms), prophecy, and other matters both of the heart of God and the heart of man. These writers have intimate knowledge of God the Father and they are well acquainted with mankind's strife and antagonism. Their writings are heart-felt, passionate, and often emotional. Oftentimes, their presentations compare and contrast the upright with the hostility of the wicked, especially in the first part of the Psalms and in Proverbs. This section is a good place to begin to enrich your own relationship with the personal God. It includes the books of Job, Psalms, Proverbs, Ecclesiastes, and Song of Solomon. See the article, The Poetical Books by J. Hampton Keathley III for a comprehensive survey of these writings. See also the article, An Introduction to the Book of Psalms by David Malick for an erudite perspective on the wisdom books with emphasis on the Psalms.

For an overview of Bible periods with their judges, kings, prophets and apostles, see Timeline of the Bible by Sunday School Resources. See also the works of Dr. Floyd Nolen Jones for a scholarly look at Bible chronology. Or google, *bible prophets and kings timeline*, for other powerful resources.

Other than showing an attractive picture of Bible divisions, what is the point of this chart? What is the big deal? Well, that circle immediately below Deuteronomy is pointing back to Deuteronomy. That is, the reader must have sufficient knowledge of the content of Deuteronomy in order to appreciate the message of the Old Testament. If one knows Deuteronomy well (and the rest of the Pentateuch), and one studies the Old Testament Scriptures that follow Deuteronomy very carefully, one will observe that as the events unfold, the reader is supposed to evaluate the acts of the people in comparison to Deuteronomy (the covenant) in order to appreciate God's covenantal response. The text includes sufficient facts for the reader to identify the relevant covenant provisions. God's people should behave according to what Deuteronomy (and the rest of the Pentateuch) says. They made a covenant with the Almighty, all knowing God. He expects them to keep that covenant just as He does.

The Bible student should well note that God keeps His entire covenant – the blessings as well as all the curses (Reference Deuteronomy chapters 27, 28 and 30). For example, in the first two chapters of 1 Samuel, we see God addressing major covenant issues with the priest and his two sons at Shiloh. Throughout 1 Samuel, we observe the outworking of many covenant issues. At the end of this chapter, see the chart, Examples of Deuteronomy in 1 Samuel, showing selected issues in 1 Samuel and the applicable covenant passages in the book of Deuteronomy, etc. These examples are provided to encourage you to observe the many covenant violations addressed in the history books and in the prophets during your Bible study. And as you observe them, take particular note of God's reaction. The story of King Solomon is a prominent example.

In the Kings, when we observe King Solomon, we see that Solomon loved women. Right? Nobody is going to argue against the fact that Solomon loved women. Solomon loved women! He loved them so much that he had 700 wives and 300 concubines (1 Kings 11). The Bible makes a big deal about that. Back in Deuteronomy 17:17, God commanded that the king shall not "multiply wives for himself, lest his heart turn away" after their gods. As we look at the Scriptures on King Solomon, we read that Solomon was the wisest man to ever live. And yet, Solomon, the wisest man, multiplied wives when God had commanded him not to. Not only that, God appeared to Solomon twice about this matter. But he would not listen. Therefore, God wants the reader to take note of this disobedience of the world's wisest man in spite of God's commandment in Deuteronomy 17 and in spite of God's personal appeal to Him. The reader should observe how that disobedience caused Solomon to stray from his extremely jealous God to embrace the gods of his many wives. Solomon's actions were also a violation of the first of the Ten Commandments: "You shall have no other gods before Me" (Exodus chapter 20). Therefore, Solomon was obliged to suffer the consequences of his disobedience – "Now the Lord was angry with Solomon because his heart was turned away from the Lord" (1 Kings 11:1-13). Remember, God keeps His entire covenant with His children, the blessings and the curses, just as we should be doing with our own children.

The New Testament

Continuing on to the last circle in our chart, we enter the New Testament; much of which is directing the reader back (pointing back or referring) to Deuteronomy and the remaining Pentateuch through the voice of the prophets. The Bible invites the reader to evaluate the New Testament events and stories, especially those in the Gospels, through the lens of the Old Testament, particularly through the prophets to Deuteronomy. God expects the reader to come to the New Testament with knowledge of the Old Covenant and Israel's failures in keeping it. The Bible student should also be acquainted with the many prophecies and promises made over thousands of years, in order to observe their fulfillment, especially in the Gospels. These fulfillments testify to the veracity of God's Word. See the article, <u>Messianic Prophecies</u> by J. Hampton Keathley III for a discussion on fulfilled prophecies.

Theologians have said that Jesus quoted the book of Deuteronomy more than any other Old Testament book. That suggests to me that Jesus was pointing the hearers of His day (and subsequent readers) back to Deuteronomy as well. This indicates that New Testament Gospel events should not have been a surprise to knowledgeable people of Jesus' day. Bible students, whose hearts were truly His, should have recognized Jesus as the promised Messiah.

In Summary

To summarize what we are saying, the first four books of the Bible are pointing to Deuteronomy, and beyond. Deuteronomy summarizes or condenses the main points of emphasis of the first four books. Deuteronomy reiterates and emphasizes the type of relationship God's people (Jews and Christians), His children, are to have with Him, and with each other. Subsequent Old Testament books are looking back and evaluating the events and actions of the people of God in contrast to the Deuteronomic covenant and the remainder of the Pentateuch. The subsequent Old Testament books also show us how the actions of God's people and their kings affect His heart; and how God responds according to His heart and the covenant. Revisit the chart,

<u>Examples of Deuteronomy in 1 Samuel</u> for a sampling of the "look-back" concept. In the book of 1 Samuel as in other Old Testament books, the author provides sufficient details for the reader to appreciate the gravity of the actions of each person or group (e.g., Hannah versus the sons of Eli, etc.) by identifying the applicable covenant provision(s). Use the sampling to gather an understanding of this concept as it appears in 1 Samuel which you should apply to all the Old Testament books that follow Deuteronomy. As you observe the covenant issues in your Bible studies, keep in mind that God can be trusted to keep His entire covenant even though His people fail to keep theirs.

The New Testament is looking back to the Old Testament and is interpreting and explaining the Old Testament through the events that are occurring in the New Testament period in light of the first appearance (or advent) of Jesus, the Christ (God's Messiah). The Gospels paint a picture of the person and works of the Bible's central character – Jesus of Nazareth. The historical book of Acts documents the obedience, trials, and spiritual battles of the apostles (and new converts) in carrying out Jesus' final instructions in Matthew 28:16-20, commonly known as the Great Commission. The doctrinal books (epistles or letters) are addressing disagreements, issues and events in the various churches, as they are occurring, in light of the teachings of Jesus, the Old Testament, and recent New Testament historical events. The doctrinal books also provide encouragement and shed light on many precepts related to the Christian walk.

Here is a statement you should write down and commit to memory. Meditate and pray on it often until its meaning is well anchored in your spirit. Then observe its wisdom and truth as you read and study your Bible:

The New is in the Old proclaimed. The Old is in the New explained (Source unknown).

Are you asking yourself, "What does that mean?" Well, the New Testament events and teachings are proclaimed (or prophesied) in the Old Testament. The fulfillment of Old Testament prophecies and promises is documented and explained in the New Testament. Therefore, one will see in the New Testament many (some say as many as 300 or more) quotes, paraphrases, or allusions to the Old Testament text. I believe there are more. See the article, New Testament Use of the Old Testament by Roger Nicole for a brief discussion.

BIBLE DIVISIONS

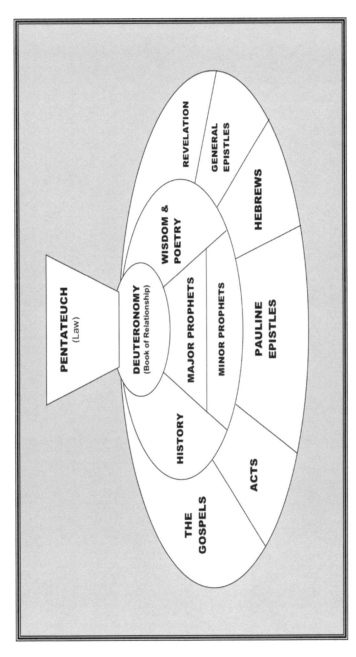

PENTATEUCH
(Law)

DEUTERONOMY
(Book of Relationship)

WISDOM &
POETRY

REVELATION

GENERAL
EPISTLES

HEBREWS

MAJOR PROPHETS

MINOR PROPHETS

PAULINE
EPISTLES

HISTORY

THE
GOSPELS

ACTS

You shall love the Lord your God with all your heart, and with all your soul, and with all your mind.
A new commandment I give to you, that you love one another, even as I have loved you (NASB).

Examples of Deuteronomy in 1 Samuel

No.	1 Samuel	Action	Deuteronomy	Evaluation
1	1:1-11	Prayer: If God would only give her a son, Hannah vows to give him to the Lord all his days.	23:21-23	Hannah could have asked for a son without a vow. Now she is obliged to perform it.
2	1:19-28, 2:11	Hannah pays her vow to the Lord just as she promised.	23:21-23, Numbers 30:1-16	When you vow to the Lord, you shall not delay to pay it.
3	1:3, 2:12-17, 2:27-36, 4:12-22	The sons of Eli, the priest, took any piece of meat before it was cooked and before the fat was burned. Eli's sons had no regard for the Lord. Eli failed to train and discipline his sons. Therefore, Eli and his two sons are cut off on the same day.	6:4-9 18:3-5, Lev 7:22-27, Lev 7:31-34,	God specified the priest's portion. But they took any portion. No one is to eat fat. Fathers are to teach their children diligently. The Lord keeps His entire covenant: the blessings and the curses.
4	7:3-14	Israel setup Baals and the Ashtaroth (idols) to serve other gods.	4:23-31 13:1-18 30:1-18	Israel served other gods and provoked the anger of God. But, when they returned to God with their whole heart, He came to their assistance to deliver them in war.
5	8:1-3	Samuel, God's priest, appointed his unrighteous sons to be judges after him. They took bribes and perverted justice.	16:18-20	God commanded judges to judge with righteous judgment. They are not to take bribes, etc.
6	8:4-22 12:19-25	The people demanded a king like the nations around them. They rejected God as their king. The people asked Samuel to pray for them because of this evil.	17:14-20	The people rejected God to have a king over them like the nations in spite of the demanding requirements of their king. Speaks to the heart of the people.
7	15:1-33	The king and the people spared Agag and the best of the sheep, oxen, etc. even though the word of the Lord through Samuel instructed them to spare no person or thing, even children.	20:16-18	The king rebelled against God for all the inhabitants of Amalek were to be utterly destroyed. Everything that breathed was to be killed.

67

New Testament: A Fresh Perspective

In our third chart – <u>New Testament Subdivisions</u> – (end of chapter) we present the layout of the New Testament from a fresh perspective. Across the top, we have columns labeled *History*, *Doctrine*, and *Prophecy*. Under *History*, we have the Gospels and the Acts of the Apostles. It appears that the book of Luke presents the chronology of the gospel events. We concluded this because of what Luke says in chapter 1, verse 3 – "in consecutive order". Other authors have a different view on the translation of this verse. It appears that the book of Acts also presents its events in chronological order. See for example the chart, <u>Chronology of Acts and the Epistles</u> by B. W. Johnson.

Under *Doctrine*, we list the letters written by the apostle Paul (Pauline Epistles) that are named for their recipients and the general letters titled according to their authors' name. The book of Hebrews is the one exception. The author of Hebrews is unknown. Some speculate that the author is the apostle Paul.

Finally, under *Prophecy*, we have apocalyptic end time events in the book of Revelation. Except for minor quotations, our present series does not address the book of Revelation.

Portrait of the Father

The Gospels – Matthew, Mark, Luke, and John – provide four perspectives of the Bible's star character: Jesus of Nazareth. The dominant character in the Old Testament is God, the Father, Who prophesies the Son. The focus of the Gospels is Jesus of Nazareth – His person and works – Who made the Father known to us. Looking back through the prophets and the Psalms, even to the book of Genesis, the Gospels provide more than ample evidence that Jesus is the Son of God and the promised Messiah (or Christ). See the article, Why God Became Man by Lehman Strauss.

Matthew identifies Jesus as the promised Messiah and king, as well as the Son of God. See the article, Lesson 1: The Genealogy Of The Promised King (Matthew 1:1-17) by David Anderson.

See also the article, Interpreting Prophecy Today – Part 3: The New Testament Doctrine of the Kingdom by John F. Walvoord.

Mark points to Jesus as the Son and Servant of God (Mark 1:1, 10:45). See the articles, Authority and Servanthood in the Gospel of Mark, Part III and Authority and Servanthood in the Gospel of Mark CONCLUSION!, both by Terri Darby Moore.

Luke presents Jesus as the Son of Man (In Hebrew: "ben adam", son of Adam, i.e., human). In Luke, Jesus refers to Himself approximately 26 times as "the Son of Man", the ruler of all mankind (Daniel 7:13-14, Luke 21:25-27). For a deeper understanding of the term, see the article, The Son of Man in the Teachings of Jesus – Is He Human or Divine? by Dr. Brad Young, president, the Gospel Research Foundation, Inc.

In the Gospel of John, the writer takes a unique approach. Starting in the very first verse, the author directs the reader's attention back to the beginning of creation in Genesis chapters 1 through 6. John purposed that the reader would come to behold and believe Jesus' and mankind's true nature. The image John presents is that Jesus is the Son of God in the midst of His own creation. But that creation is so far from God that they do not know Him nor recognize Jesus as their Creator. Even His own people (Israel) did not receive Him (John 1:1-18).

A major part of Jesus' mission on earth was to reveal the Father to this dark, sin-filled world. His means or approach to accomplish this was to display Himself as *the true image of God*. Therefore, Jesus went about doing works that exemplified His Father's nature and character – the Father's image as presented in the Old Testament. Consequently, the temple rulers and teachers of that day should have recognized Him by His words and His deeds as the prophesied *Messiah* bringing light into darkness (Isaiah 9:2, John 8:12) and as the promised *Prophet* speaking the words the Father had put in His mouth (Deuteronomy 18:15-19, John 8:26-28, 12:44-50). The words and works of Jesus were intentionally designed to send forth a very strong and undeniable message regarding Himself (being in the form of a man) in comparison to that of the invisible God. His goal was to reveal God the Father by demonstrating that He Himself is the true visible image of the invisible God (Colossians 1:15-16, Hebrews 1:1-4). He did all this so that the world might come to believe God instead of the lies emanating from the devil. Therefore, the reader is to see the words and works of Jesus as painting a portrait of the Father of the Old Testament, especially as He presents Himself in Exodus 34:5-9 and as confirmed by Jesus in John 17:6-8.

So what portrait did Jesus convey regarding the Father? Exodus 34:5-9 is a passage I like to refer to as the image – nature and character – of God:

"5And the LORD descended in the cloud and stood there with him [Moses] as he called upon the name of the LORD. 6Then the LORD passed by in front of him and proclaimed, "The LORD, the LORD God, *compassionate* and *gracious, slow to anger,* and *abounding in lovingkindness and truth; 7Who* keeps lovingkindness for thousands, *Who forgives iniquity, transgression and sin*; yet He will by no means leave the guilty unpunished, visiting the iniquity of fathers on the children and on the grandchildren to the third and fourth generations." 8And Moses made haste to bow low toward the earth and worship. 9And he said, "If now I have found favor in Your sight, O Lord, I pray, let the Lord go along in our midst, even though the people are so obstinate; and do You pardon our iniquity and our sin, and take us as Your own possession." (Exodus 34:5-9) [Brackets and Italics mine].

In this passage, the words are directly from the mouth of God speaking to Moses, the obedient prophet and servant of God. This passage presents the following portrait of what God, the Father, is truly like:

The Father is compassionate – The word "compassion" is used 92 times in the Bible, 75 of them in the Old Testament, where we see the image, the character and heart of God the Father on display. In addition, the Bible uses the word "compassionate" 13 times, most of them referring to the nature of God the Father, all of which are in the Old Testament. Jesus demonstrated the compassion of the Father when He fed the 5,000 (Mark 6:33-44) and the 4,000 (Mark 8:1-9). "And seeing the multitudes, He felt compassion for them, because they were distressed and downcast like sheep without a shepherd" (Matthew 9:36). He also portrayed the Father's compassion in healing any number of diseases as in Matthew chapters 8 and 9.

The Father is gracious – Jesus showed forth the grace (unmerited favor and power) of the Father with the woman caught in adultery (John 8:1-11); with the Apostle Paul on the Damascus road (Acts 22:6-16), also with those who believe on His name even to this day through His self-sacrifice for our sins (John 3:16-21, Romans 5:1-17 and 6:20-23, Ephesians 3:1-13). For an in-depth discussion on grace, see the Auburn University article, The Grace of God. See also the three articles The Grace of God, Part I, II, and III from the series, Fundamentals of the Faith by Bob Deffinbaugh.

The Father is slow to anger – In all of His encounters with the scribes and Pharisees, Jesus seldom displayed any anger, even when the scribes and Pharisees conspired to kill him, though He had violated no law and done no wrong (Matthew 12, <u>John 8:39-40</u>). For an extended study of God's anger in both the Old and New Testaments, see the article, <u>The Wrath of God In The New Testament: Never Against His New Covenant Community</u> by James M. Arlandson.

The Father is abounding in lovingkindness – He keeps lovingkindness to a thousand generations of those who love Him. The Bible tells us in John 1 that "He [Jesus] was in the world, and the world was made through Him, and the world did not know Him. He came to His own [the Jews], and those who were His own did not receive Him" (vv10-11). Yet, these are the very same people for whom Jesus willingly sacrificed Himself on a cross, because He loved them and us with an everlasting, unconditional love (<u>1 John 4:7-11</u>). The Bible translators coined the word "lovingkindness" to describe the idea in the Old Testament original language of an everlasting loyal, selfless, undeserved, and unconditional love. See <u>Definition of Hebrew For Lovingkindness</u> on the Precept Austin website. It appears in the Bible 176 times, all of them in the Old Testament, beginning in Genesis. The last entry is in the book of Jonah, 4:2, which states quite well who Jonah considered God to be. Jesus taught His disciples, "Greater love has no one than this, that one lay down his life for his friends" (John 15:13). And that is exactly what Jesus did for His friends and even His enemies (Romans 5:10).

The Father is abounding in truth – In Matthew, Jesus preached His longest sermon that we know as the Sermon on the Mount (Matthew 5 – 7), revealing such great heavenly truths that the crowd was amazed. "The result was that when Jesus had finished these words, the multitudes were amazed at His teaching; for He was teaching them as one having authority, and not as their scribes" (Matthew 7:28-29). Jesus taught heavenly truths, as in John 14 – 17, that the world does not know because the prince of this world "is a liar and the father of lies" (John 8:43-46). The world rejects the truth and accepts the lie. How about you?

The Father is forgiving – Who "forgives iniquity, transgression, and sin" as in Jesus forgiving the paralytic in Mark 2:1-12 and Matthew 9:1-8. Jesus said to the immoral woman who washed His feet with her tears and wiped them with her hair, "Your sins have been forgiven" (Luke 7:36-50). "Truly I say to you, all sins shall be forgiven the sons of men, and whatever blasphemies they utter; but whoever blasphemes against the Holy Spirit never has forgiveness, but is guilty of an eternal sin" (Mark 3:28-29). Jesus taught extensively on the concept of forgiveness to confirm the Father's heart as expressed in the Old Testament.

Yet He [the Father] will by no means leave the guilty unpunished – In the end, God will uphold the requirements of His justice system and punish the lawless. Jesus attempted to convince the scribes and Pharisees of who He is. Claiming to know God, they rejected Jesus out of hand. Therefore Jesus said to them, "You know neither Me, nor My Father". "I said therefore to you, that you shall die in your sins; for unless you *believe* that I am He, you shall die in your sins" (John 8:19-24). They were guilty of not believing God. Jesus' response to Nicodemus was that, "He who *believes* in Him [Jesus] is not judged; he who does not *believe* has been judged already, because he has not *believed* in the name of the only begotten Son of God" (John

3:18). John the Baptist testified for the benefit of all saying, "He who *believes* in the Son has eternal life; but he who *does not obey* the Son shall not see life, but the wrath of God abides on him" (John 3:36) [Italics mine].

Exodus 34:5-9 is indeed one of the key Old Testament passages that Jesus used to guide His ministry as He went about doing the work the Father sent Him to do. Oftentimes, Jesus reminded His disciples of what they were observing and what they were experiencing when He said, "I and the Father are one" (John 10:30). "He who has seen Me has seen the Father" (John 14:9).

In the High Priestly Prayer, Jesus confirms to the Father that His portrait is complete – "I manifested Thy name to the men whom Thou gavest Me out of the world." "For the words which Thou gavest Me I have given to them; and they received them, and truly understood that I came forth from Thee, and they believed that Thou didst send Me" (John 17:6, 8). Much of what we know of His name is contained in Exodus 34:5-9. It is the passage quoted throughout the Old Testament to describe the heart and character of God. And it is this passage that helps us know how God will act and react in the lives of those who believe Jesus.

The Holy Spirit at Work

The book of Acts describes for us how those who believed Jesus – His twelve apostles and the other disciples – worked diligently and courageously to make disciples according to Jesus' commandment to spread the good news of forgiveness of sin and the promise of eternal life all over the world (Matthew 28:16-20).

While the focus is their efforts, the main character (or power) is the Holy Spirit. In the power and person of the Holy Spirit, the apostles made new disciples and trained them to carry on their work after they were gone. They established churches, appointed elders and deacons, and provided theological guidance. In the midst of unrelenting satanic attacks that continue even today, they boldly proclaimed the Gospel, prayed fervently, and enthusiastically provided passionate encouragement to the new believers while sacrificing their own comfort and even their own lives, just as their Master had done.

See the article, The Historical Books of the New Testament by J. Hampton Keathley III for a comprehensive introduction to the Gospels and Acts. See also, The Unique Contribution of the Book of Acts by Bob Deffinbaugh who presents an intriguing perspective of the Acts of the Apostles. See as well, A Study Outline of Acts by Greg Herrick.

Christian Doctrine

As we return to our chart – New Testament Subdivisions – following the history books, we have the column labeled *Doctrine*. These are doctrinal epistles (or letters) providing theological precepts and principles and addressing other issues in the church. The chronicle of the Acts of the Apostles introduces many of the peoples and places that we encounter in the books containing doctrine. In the chart, Chronology of Acts and the Epistles by B. W. Johnson, note the integration of the doctrinal epistles with the chronology of events in the book of Acts.

Now, what's going on in the doctrinal epistles is this. The

doctrinal books (epistles or letters) are addressing issues and circumstances in the various churches, as they are occurring. The author provides his response in light of the teachings of Jesus, the Old Testament, and recent New Testament historical events. In the Gospels, the authors have presented many facts to prove that Jesus is the prophesied Messiah-King. Jesus has demonstrated by word and deed that He is the promised Prophet; but most importantly, He is the Son of God. Not only that, He is the sacrificial "Lamb of God" Who pays the penalty for the sins of the whole world by willingly and obediently offering Himself as a brutal sacrifice to God for all mankind of all ages. Jesus has laid out what He has come to do, what the kingdom of God is all about, and what He expects of His apostles and disciples after He is gone. He has commissioned the Apostles to go out and establish the church by spreading the Gospel – the good news of Jesus' sacrifice, death, burial, and *resurrection*, the forgiveness of sin, and the promise of eternal life – to all nations and tongues.

Following Jesus' *resurrection* and *ascension*, the apostles waited for the outpouring of the promised Holy Spirit Who came upon them in Acts chapter 2 to indwell them (John 14:16-17). In obedience to Christ, His apostles went forth to spread the Gospel and establish churches. As this is going on, just like you would expect if we were starting a church here and now, in time, we would have doctrinal (theological precepts and principles) questions and behavioral issues to come up. We would likely have conflict to resolve because of questions and debates. Someone might say, "I don't think that's the way it ought to be done." "I remember Jesus taught thus and so." "He didn't explain it the way you're talking about doing it." "Well, that's not what I believe!"

Or whatever. Because our objective is to rescue souls from the domain of darkness, there will be resistance from the prince of darkness (i.e. Satan).

So then, the biblical author, like Paul for example, is dealing with issues as they come up in the churches he established. In response to these issues, the author is saying, when we look at the Old Testament and the life and teachings of Jesus, plus what I have personally heard from the Holy Spirit, this is what God has said. This is what we should be doing. This is what you should believe, and how you should behave. Christ has called us to be a peculiar people in the eyes of the world. We are to live our lives according to Kingdom values not the values of the world. Looking back at the Old Testament, this is why Jesus said what He did and why He did the things He did.

The doctrinal books, then, are looking back at the Old Testament and the gospels to say this is who Jesus is. This is what He taught and commanded. Therefore, as disciples (followers) of Jesus, we should act and speak as Jesus did; and this is how we ought to be responding to the issues at hand. Jesus is our example. Therefore, the epistles (or letters) contain the apostles' response and instructions concerning questions from, and issues and problems in the various churches that they had worked so diligently to establish and now to maintain.

Unfortunately, for today's reader, the author does not generally provide a clear statement of the issues addressed. The people to whom the author wrote the letters knew the questions and issues. So the author did not have to state them. Consequently, today's reader, through careful study, must deduce the problem or issue from the author's response to the unstated problem or issue – i.e., observe how the author addresses subject matters in the letter. Then figure out what the problems or issues are and write them out. From this detail study, one can identify or derive godly precepts and principles to *govern* the way we *actually live* our lives today.

Included in the doctrinal letters are three books – 1 and 2 Timothy and Titus – referred to as Pastoral Epistles. In addition to dealing with doctrinal and theological and behavioral issues, these books address church order and functions. Specific instructions provide guidance on the qualifications of elders and deacons and in church ministry. See the article, Chapter Five: Literary And Theological Context of 1 Timothy 2:15 by Terri Darby Moore.

For a brief survey of all books in the New Testament, with book theme and purpose, see the articles published under the general title, Concise New Testament Survey by J. Hampton Keathley III.

Four Major Characters

There are four major human characters spanning the Old and New Testaments – **Abraham**, **Moses**, **David**, and **Jesus**. The Bible invites us to focus on what it emphasizes regarding each of these characters.

Speaking of **Abraham**, whose name was Abram before God changed it, the Old Testament Scriptures tell us, "Then he [Abram] believed in the Lord; and He [God] reckoned it to him as righteousness" (Genesis 15:6). [Brackets mine]. The New Testament quotes this passage in three different books – Romans 4:3, 9, Galatians 3:6, and James 2:23 – with emphasis on the fact that Abraham "believed God". Why is this important? We have only to refer back to Genesis chapter 3 for the contrast. Adam and Eve's actions say they did not believe God. As a result, the whole earth population ended up completely separated from God. So God found Himself a man in the person of Abraham who would believe Him and obey Him. When you consider this fact within the context of the corruption of mankind (Genesis chapters 6 and 11), the Abraham character is even more striking.

We see the name, **Moses**, appearing 792 times in the Bible, 79 times in the New Testament. We also see Jesus compared to Moses in Hebrews 3:1-3 where Scripture informs us that Moses was faithful in all God's house, and so was Jesus (to confirm God's promise in Deuteronomy 18:15, quoted below). When God appointed him to deliver the children of Israel out of the hand of slavery in Egypt, "Moses said to God, 'Who am I, that I should go to Pharaoh, and that I should bring the sons of Israel out of Egypt?'" God responded saying, "Certainly I will be with you, and this shall be the sign to you that it is I Who have sent you: when you have brought the people out of Egypt, you shall worship God at this mountain" (Exodus 3:11-12). Obviously, Moses believed God would be with him. Moses' faithfulness stemmed from the fact that he "believed God" would be faithful to His Word. Therefore, he committed himself wholeheartedly to the mission of God so that, until Jesus, "no prophet has risen in Israel like Moses, whom the Lord knew face to face" (Deuteronomy 34:10).

When it comes to **David**, one has only to read the story of David and Goliath (1 Samuel 17) to appreciate the fact that David "believed and he trusted God". Deuteronomy and Joshua stressed that the army of God is not to fear, for God will be with them, to deliver them (e.g., Deuteronomy 3:21-22, 31:8). Yet fear immobilized the whole of King Saul's army. David's willingness to battle Goliath demonstrated he truly believed God would be with Him. In addition to that, David had a "heart" for God and for the things of God. David walked before the Lord. Yes, he had his shortcomings, but his relationship with his God governed the way he lived his life. We see this in the books of Samuel, 1 Kings, and throughout the Psalms of David. God was so impressed with David that He promised him that his descendant would rule over the earth forever. To emphasize David's relationship and God's promise, the Scriptures refer to Jesus (the eternal King of kings and Lord of lords) as "the Son of David" as in David's descendant. In fact, we see in the very first verse of the book of Matthew (the first book of the New Testament) that Scripture ties three of these four characters together – "THE book of the genealogy of Jesus Christ, the son of David, the son of Abraham". God first called Abraham to begin His program in the world. His last called of the four is **Jesus**, the beginning and the end, forever.

Throughout the Old Testament, **Jesus** is mentioned, alluded to, promised, and prophesied. The coming Messiah, the anointed One of God, the Holy One of Israel, the eternal King and High Priest, is a major thread throughout the Old Testament beginning in Genesis 3:15 as the "seed" of the woman. The term "Messiah" refers to the Anointed Savior or Liberator of the world from the "domain of darkness".

On the night before His crucifixion, the high priest questioned Jesus, "saying to Him, 'Are You the Christ [Messiah], the Son of the Blessed One [God]?' And Jesus said, 'I am; and you shall see the Son of Man sitting at the right hand of Power, and coming with the clouds of heaven'" (Mark 14:61-62). In this passage, Jesus has declared Himself to be the prophesied Messiah, the Son of God, and thereby He was also declaring Himself to be the Savior of the world Who was obedient to the Father, even to death on a cross.

In Deuteronomy 18:15-18, we read, "The Lord your God will raise up for you a prophet like me [Moses] from among you, from your countrymen, you shall listen to him. This is according to all that you asked of the Lord your God in Horeb on the day of the assembly, saying, "Let me not hear again the voice of the Lord my God, let me not see this great fire anymore, lest I die.' And the Lord said to me, 'They have spoken well. I will raise up a *prophet* from among their countrymen like you [Moses], and I will put My words in his mouth, and he shall speak to them all that I commanded him.'" On more than one occasion in the book of John, Jesus informs His listeners that He speaks what He heard His Father say. And He does the deeds He saw His Father do. And as the Father has given Him commandment, so He does. What Jesus was attempting to get His listeners to appreciate is that He speaks and acts exactly like the prophesied *Prophet* of Deuteronomy 18.

You may be asking yourself, "So what is the significance or connection between these four major characters?" Well, think about it. Adam and Eve did not believe God or they simply rebelled against Him (1 Timothy 2:14) and plunged (i.e., predestined) all mankind to a world replete with sin, conflict and hostility, and to eternal existence in hell. Mankind lost its connection to God. Mankind turned completely away from God to seek idols made with hands. In Genesis 15, God told Abram (Abraham) that he would have a son in his old age, even though his wife was *barren* and beyond childbearing age; and that his descendants would be too numerous to count. At that time, Abram was 75 and Sarai (Sarah, his wife) was 65 years old. They had no children. Yet Abram believed God anyway even though it took God 25 years to fulfill His promise. So when Abram demonstrated that he "believed God" would keep His promise based solely on God's word, that was a very big deal. David likewise believed God based solely on His word, as did Moses and Jesus. And their lives reflect their belief. Believing God based solely on His word is still a big deal to God even today. The Bible asks mankind (you and me) to "believe Jesus" in order to be saved from the wrath of God to come. Remember, God is faithful to keep His word. Look for this thread – the question of believing and disbelieving God – throughout the Bible. It is especially prevalent in the book of John where the word "believe" appears 49 times.

Finally, all four characters served as the mediator between God and man, Jesus being the final and eternal Mediator for the whole of mankind for all eternity. So why not submit yourself totally to Him today for God has declared that the day is coming when you will, whether willing or not – "And being found in appearance as a man, He [Jesus] humbled Himself by becoming obedient to the point of death, even death on a cross. 9Therefore also God [the Father] highly exalted Him, and bestowed on Him the name which is above every name, 10that at the name of Jesus EVERY KNEE SHOULD BOW, of those who are in heaven, and on earth, and under the earth, 11and that every tongue should confess that Jesus Christ is Lord, to the glory of God the Father." (Philippians 2:8-11) [Brackets mine].

So, what questions did we stir up in you thus far? Write them down now. Also include any reaction to what you have read thus far. And as your questions are answered, document the answers next to your questions. Hopefully, by the time you get to the end of the series, many of your questions will have been answered; and you will be inspired to study your Bible daily, and more diligently, to discover for yourself the answers for most of the questions that remain.

New Testament Subdivisions

History	Doctrine	Prophecy

Gospels

Four views of
the person and work
of Jesus Christ

Matthew -The King
Mark   -The Servant
Luke   -Son of Man
John   -Son of God

Pauline Epistles

Romans	1 Thessalonians
1 Corinthians	2 Thessalonians
2 Corinthians	1 Timothy
Galatians	2 Timothy
Ephesians	Titus
Philippians	Philemon
Colossians	

Revelation

A. Vision of the Christ
B. The seven
    churches
C. The period of
    tribulation
D. Second coming of
    the Christ
E. Millennial reign of the
    Christ
F. Great White Throne
    Judgment
G. The new heaven
    and the new earth
H. Final words from
    Jesus Christ

Acts of the Apostles

Person and work
of the Holy Spirit

Birth and early history
of the church by the
apostles through the
work of the Holy Spirit

Hebrews & General Epistles

Hebrews

General Epistles

James	1 John
1 Peter	2 John
2 Peter	3 John
	Jude

Part 2

Context

*Many other signs therefore Jesus also performed
in the presence of the disciples, which are not
written in this book; but these have been written
that you may believe that Jesus is the Christ, the
Son of God; and that believing you may have life
in His name.*
John 20:30-31

Understanding Context

When confronting a complex subject, have you ever heard the phrase, "just give me the big picture"? In this instance, we are talking about sparing me the details. Provide me a minimal summary instead. The Bible is a huge volume with many divisions, subdivisions, periods, and books. How does one begin to discover its life-saving, life-giving, Kingdom message? How do I condense all its pages down to a single concept that my finite mind can grasp and visualize?

The Big Picture

How do I identify that one thing that would provide a context from which to relate all other things? If I could just find that one thing, the one powerful thing that speaks to the whole of the Bible, perhaps that would lead to one more powerful thing, to another, and so on. Then I would be on my way to getting my head around God's Holy Scriptures. This was my struggle until the heart attack; one of the things I talked to God about during my recovery. The conversation went something like this: God, I am having trouble understanding what the simple message of the Bible is. You know how my mind works. You know I need to be able to understand and describe it in a simple way. I would like to know what the Bible is about in one or two sentences, three at the most. So Father, please, show me what the Bible is about in the least number of sentences. A few days passed before He gave me His response. But He did answer me with a "hallelujah" moment! As only my heavenly Father can do, He told me what the Bible is actually all about in a single word. He said, *"Relationship*. And relationship is the most important thing to you". Did you catch that? Don't miss it! God has explained what the Bible is about in one word! OK! I hear your mind spinning right now. "What did God mean by that?" Don't worry. I had the same question!

To answer our question, let's take a stroll back to Genesis. When God created Adam and Eve, in addition to populating the earth, He created them to have *relationship* with Him. He regularly visited His creation. In Genesis 3, after the man and his wife had committed the sin, we read, "And they [Adam and Eve] heard the sound of the Lord God walking in the garden in the cool of the day and they hid themselves" (v8). God came to visit the crown jewel of His new creation, I suspect, as He had done on many previous occasions. He chose the best time of the day – "in the cool of the day" – to sit around and visit. But His crowning joy had committed the one act that would destroy that relationship. They had disobeyed God's single command not to eat of that one tree. God's plan had been to have billions of Adam's and Eve's, in

His image, according to His likeness, emulating Him, and covering the entire earth. He could visit them regularly so they could experience the ecstasy of His presence at any time. Their disobedience threw a monkey wrench – a disruption or sabotage – into God's plan. As a result, God lost not only His relationship with Adam and Eve, who lost the utter joy of His presence with them; but God also lost His relationship with all the billions of their descendants, including most of the seven billion living today. God wants to get back what He lost.

In the final analysis, the Bible is really all about God putting His family back together and building an intimate love relationship in preparation for an eternal, joy-filled future we cannot now comprehend. Everything in the Bible takes place within the context of the originally created image and likeness of God in Adam and Eve, before their sin and its consequences (Genesis 3), and God regaining His personal possession from the deceiver, i.e., Satan (Luke 19:10).

OK! I hear you! You want to know why is it taking God so long and what has He been doing for the last six thousand years? Right? I would love to talk to you about that. But it will have to wait for a future lesson – i.e., a future book. For now, we are trying to get a handle on the big picture, which will provide a context for understanding the details of God's Word – the magnificent gift He has given to the world. And it is truly an amazingly magnificent gift. We would never know Him nor would we ever truly know ourselves. Therefore, He tells us about Himself and He tells us about ourselves. And He tells us how to fix our own dysfunctional relationships because *relationship* is the most important thing to us.

The Meaning of Context

In many Bible study programs, authors frequently give attention to two types of context, 1) the historical-cultural, and 2) the literary context including genre and surrounding text. TheFreeDictionary.com defines context as, "1) The part of a text or statement that surrounds a particular word or passage and determines its meaning, or 2) the parts of a piece of writing, speech, etc., that precede and follow a word or passage and contribute to its full meaning." All of this is important. However, for the purpose of our study, we shall think of context first as a "dome" covering the entire Bible from beginning to end – the big picture. Second, we shall think of context as "related text" that may surround the passage, but could come well before and far after a particular study passage or book. "Related text" adds to, expounds on, or explains the study passage. To help you understand and appreciate the significance of our definition, consider the layout of the Bible. That is, consider its various subdivisions and how often they relate to the same period of time, characters, events, and/or subject matter. Consider, for example, the appearance of Jesus, in the Gospels, Who was prophesied in the Prophets and even in the Pentateuch. You should *always* keep the overall context – the big picture ("dome") and "related text" – in mind as you study your Bible. Much confusion and misinterpretation can occur when you don't.

History and Prophecy

Think of the Bible as a history book of man's existence on the earth written by the One who created it for His purpose and Who providentially presides over it all. Think of it also as a prophetic book written by the One Who declares the end from the beginning to prove His existence to us. Satan wants you to believe there is no God. So he has placed all sorts of schemes before us to deceive us. Too many of us believe there is no God! These Satan expects to keep in his domain. Therefore, God has given us prophesies and their fulfillments as irrefutable evidence that He exists. He is the Almighty, all knowing God! And His purpose will be accomplished (Isaiah 46:9-11). He starts His book at the beginning of time and ends it at the termination of the current age, the last days. Your's could be the generation to see the culmination of God's plan.

God wants us first to view that history through various *windows*. Therefore, He compiled the Bible's 66 books not in chronological order but according to each window's *viewpoint*. Viewpoint is, "a position from which something is observed or considered; the mental attitude that determines a person's opinions or judgments" (thefreedictionary.com/viewpoint). Imagine yourself on the outside looking through the window of a vacant home. Looking through a bathroom window provides one viewpoint, usually a limited one. But looking through a family room window allows one to see more of the home, perhaps even the dining room and kitchen, a broader view. In the same way, viewing the Bible from a better viewpoint enhances our understanding and improves our interpretation.

Second, God wants us to *meditate* on the whole of Scripture to *correlate* it all into a cohesive story of *cause* and *effect*. Then, He expects us to consider its significance for our own lives here on earth and throughout eternity!

Windows and Viewpoints

In many respects, the whole of the Pentateuch is the genesis of God's program. It presents the origin and development of the earth and man, and the covenant calling of Abram (Abraham) and the nation of Israel, the people of God. However, long before there was an Abraham and Israel, there was abundant trouble in the earth. The Bible introduces the tension in the first three chapters of Genesis. The drama begins to unfold immediately in the fourth chapter and it continues thereafter. In the fifth book – Deuteronomy – Moses revisits and reiterates the major points of Israel's covenant relationship with their God. The setting for this book (the context) is important because it explains the "why" for the book. Which explains why the book should be important to us today.

Forty years prior, the children of Israel had refused to trust God to cover and support them in taking possession of the land that He had promised to give them. They decided to rebel against God. In fear, they refused to go in and take possession of the land from the Canaanites. Instead, they cried out for someone to take them back to Egypt and they were saying, "Would that we had died in this wilderness!" That made God so angry that in exasperation, He cried out to Moses saying, "How long will this people spurn Me? And how long will they not believe in Me, despite all the signs which I have performed in their midst?" As punishment, God decreed that all the men of war, from twenty years old and up, surely would not enter the land He had sworn to their forefathers to give them. Therefore, God appointed 40 years of wanderings for that generation to die in the wilderness according to what they had asked (Numbers 13 – 14). This is an admonishment to us to be careful of what we ask for.

As we enter Deuteronomy, the 40 years are now up and Moses is preparing the people – mostly the younger generation now 40 years later – to go in and possess the land. Most of these men were less than 20 years old when Moses first gave the Law – The Covenant. Therefore, many may not have heard it directly from Moses and others may not have understood it. Others may have forgotten many of the details. Still others needed a stern reminder. Like a loving father sending his son or daughter off to college for the first time, from his deathbed, Moses takes this final opportunity to revisit critical subjects in the Law and to chide the Israelites to be diligent in keeping the covenant with their God; stressing the severe consequences God has already demonstrated if they don't. For God is a covenant keeping God! Covenant is a values and character issue with God. Therefore, even today, He invites us to evaluate Him in the same way He evaluates His people, based on the covenants – the Old and the New. He expects His children to trust Him and to obey Him.

The Pentateuch, providing its setting and context in Genesis 1-11, is the first window through which we view the Bible and begin to gain understanding of it.

For a quick summary of biblical covenants throughout the

Bible, see the Bible.org article, <u>The Covenants of Scripture</u>:.

The History books provide another window through which we observe how God establishes His covenant people, the nation of Israel, in the Promised Land (see Joshua); and how they matured as a nation in comparison to the culture of the surrounding nations. These books emphasize the thorny issue of the form of government for the developing nation and how that choice plays out. But the primary focus, from the viewpoint of the history books, is squarely on the issue of obedience to the covenant as clearly expressed in the books of Joshua and Judges. Therefore, one must study these books in the context of "covenant". Only through sufficient advanced knowledge of the Pentateuch (with emphasis on Deuteronomy) is one able to grasp the significant lessons of this portion of man's history. See the <u>Timeline of the Bible</u> by Sunday School Resources for further contextual period-pointers.

The Wisdom and Poetry window looks at history from a different viewpoint. This window adds a personal and relational (from the heart) context to the period of the history books. Much of its focus is on the hostility of the wicked versus the struggle of the righteous for both nations and individuals. From this vantage point, we get to observe numerous contrasts and comparisons between the upright and the wicked. It shows us how the choices of each influence relationships and life's outcome here on earth and throughout eternity. Also from this viewpoint, we learn about the person and power of God, the Father. We get to experience the manifold wisdom and heart-felt worship of God. The covenant is the backdrop for this window. The covenant distinguishes God's people from the rest of the world. So keep the covenant (especially the book of relationship) in mind as you study this important portion of the Holy Scriptures.

From the viewpoint of the Prophets' window, we gain an understanding of how the peoples' – Israel and the nations' – actions impacted God's heart. The prophets emphasize God's expectation of a faithful, obedient, covenant-love relationship that faithless Israel (including Judah) failed to provide. Instead, the Israelites were only concerned about themselves, what they wanted, what their flesh lusted after (e.g., see Jeremiah 2 – 3). This is not much different from the way we live our lives today.

To gain a deeper understanding of the context for the Prophets, the Bible student must connect the individual prophet with the reigning king or kings of his day. In the Chart of Israel's and Judah's Kings and Prophets by Craig T. Owens, the author not only delineates how the king's behavior looked to God, but he also presents the prophets who served God during the king's reign. This chart allows the Bible student to correlate the Scriptures relating to the king with the Scriptures relating to the prophet who served God during the king's reign. This chart can aid the Bible student in associating the issues addressed by God in the prophets with the historical events and actions described in the related history books – i.e., Samuel, Kings, and Chronicles. You may use the chart to identify the king and the associated prophet. Or, you may wish to go directly to the Scriptures to select your king and prophet. For example, in 2 Chronicles, observe the historical events of each king, beginning with King Hezekiah, as compared to related passages about that king in the prophets. Using a Bible study tool such as <u>biblegateway.com</u> or <u>net.bible.org</u>, (smartphone apps are *Bible Gateway* and *Lumina*, respectively) perform a search in the history books using the name of the king from 2 Chronicles (or the chart) to obtain a list of verses from the history books. Then perform a similar search in the books of the prophets to locate a list of verses from that source. Study the verses from each source in their broader context. In your study, identify and correlate the subject matter from the two sources. Then, derive and extract the setting and context for God's message given through the prophet. Then, write them out. Include the relevant covenant provisions. Apply this same approach to each of the kings and prophets. Keep in mind that the exilic and post-exilic prophets served, for the most part, during the period when Israel had lost self-rule. Therefore, they had no king or they had a puppet king who ruled over them.

In the New Testament, we have the Gospel windows, each with its own viewpoint – Jesus as king, Jesus as servant, Son of Man, Son of God. The Acts of the Apostles, following Jesus' ascension, provides another window through which we observe (a) the faithfulness of Jesus' apostles as they labored to carry out the commandments of Christ, and (b) the work of the Holy Spirit in the context of both the Old Testament and the Gospels. Finally, the Doctrinal Epistles' window shows the spiritual battles and struggles of the saints, and the instructional guidance and encouragement provided by the apostles through the continuing aid and power of the Holy Spirit.

So, in summary, what am I saying to you? I maintain that the Bible divisions and subdivisions are windows through which we observe a portion of mankind's history through the eyes of God. Through these windows, we also observe God's declaration and fulfillment of future events to prove He truly exists with all power. From various viewpoints and perspectives, all focused on the issue of "covenant" relationships (within the context of the image of God in man or the lack thereof), we see God's disappointments; and as well, we see His prophecies and plans unfold. The divisions and subdivisions enable us to get our minds around manageable ideas and concepts without being overwhelmed. Yet we should always keep in mind that the entire Bible is still one history spanning thousands of years, with accompanying prophecies and their fulfillments, leading to a single outcome.

Culture & Setting

Another view to understanding context deals with culture and setting. The writings of the various authors depend on the situation in the context of culture and setting. Therefore, our understanding of the Bible is complete only when we have at least a minimal grasp of the historical and cultural setting of the day and the immediate circumstances of the setting in which the present situation, event, or story takes place. For an introduction to the concept of setting for Bible stories and events, see the article, Israel: Understanding the Setting of the Story of the Bible by Heather Goodman. For the setting of events taking place in the New Testament, see the article Introduction and Historical Setting by Allen Ross. Also, see all the articles by Allen Ross from the series, The Religious World of Jesus for a more in-depth view.

Avoid Presuppositions

Allow me to provide a final note of caution. Many of us have quite a bit of Bible knowledge. Some of it we obtained through youth ministries and our personal study of Scripture. Other knowledge came from sermons and written messages such as books. Unfortunately, much of what we know may not conform to the context. So my caution to you is, *avoid presuppositions*. What I am suggesting that you do is, put to bed what you already know and try to come to the Scriptures with a clean slate and fresh eyes. Focus solely on what the Scripture is actually saying rather than accept what you think you already know. This is not easy, I know. For when we read a very familiar passage, we see what we have heard so many times in the past. But often times, when we slow down and take the time to read the passage very carefully, within its immediate and broader context, we obtain quite a different message. Therefore, read Scripture cautiously and reverently, *avoiding your presuppositions.*

5

An Eagle Eye View Of The Bible

Have you ever said to yourself, "I wish I had a comprehensive understanding of what the Bible is really saying?" "There are many great stories in the Bible. Nevertheless, there has to be one overarching story or message of the Bible, but what?" Here, we present the simple story of the Bible in chart form from what I call the eagle eye view of the Bible – the big picture. In other words, we know that the eagle has keen eyes and flies very high like an airplane. If you have been in an airplane, you probably have noticed that as you start coming down to land, at first, many objects on the ground are not even visible. But the closer you get to the ground, the more objects you can see. You begin to recognize tracks of land and other large objects such as the skyscrapers. You finally get to the point that you recognize the rooftops of houses and you can see the cars moving along the streets. That's the eagle eye view. When you get on the ground, things look totally different. There is an overwhelming amount of detail.

The Dome – The Bible Story

Our chart (<u>end of this chapter</u>) presents the big picture (the eagle eye view) of the Bible story. We have omitted voluminous distracting details not required for this phase of our study. Take a moment now to make a cursory review of our chart before we dive in.

Welcome back! So how are we to understand this four-part chart? Well, think of the chart as a *dome*, covering the entire Bible situated underneath it. This is the overarching essential message that Jesus wants you to understand and believe in your heart. The extreme amount of detail is excluded. But as in the airplane ride, they are still there below the dome. The layout of the chart offers a broad context for understanding and connecting Bible details.

Our chart is presented in four parts with part one containing the least detail of the story. Each succeeding part includes additional detail, with part four providing the most detail. The goal is to provide you sufficient context for understanding Bible details *from God's perspective*. Each succeeding volume in this series presents a significant thread to enhance the broader context, from God's perspective. It is my prayer that you will begin to see the Bible through the eyes of God, first and foremost; and not just look at it from a human-centered viewpoint. While the Bible is a story about man on the earth, it is more a story about God and God's compassion, grace (unmerited divine favor), and mercy (not giving what you actually deserve) in dealing with that man as would a loving father.

If not already done, please take a moment now to make a cursory review of all four parts of our chart before proceeding to our description.

Top Line / Bottom Line

This chart is adapted from the "Top Line / Bottom Line" concept of Dr. Charles Baylis, Professor of Bible Exposition, Dallas Theological Seminary. For a more in-depth understanding of the biblical story as presented by Dr. Baylis, see the Biblical Story on his website, thebiblicalstory.org.

Each of the four parts includes a subheading generally in the form of "question / answer", a contrasting top line / bottom line section, a graphical rendering of the fall and redemption of man, and a Scripture reference section at the bottom that is identical in each part. A scriptural passage makes a specific point. Each succeeding passage builds on the points made in the preceding passages. You should study the passages in the sequence presented, keeping in mind the cumulative message of the previous verses. The sequence begins in the left most block with a study of Genesis chapters 1 – 6. Then flows to the top of the first (left most) column and continues down that column over to the top of the next column, down that column to the top of the next column, and so on.

The Top Line / Bottom Line concept contrasts the image of God with the image of unregenerate (natural) man, a major Bible thread or perspective. For example, read and meditate on Psalm 1. On the top line is the image and likeness of God – righteousness, compassion, kindness, unconditional love, favor, forgiveness, mercy, justice, etc. (Exodus 34:6-7, Galatians 5:22-23). On the bottom line is the fallen nature of man – ungodliness, selfishness, pride, arrogance, anger, "lovers of pleasure rather than lovers of God", "disobedient to parents", and disobedient to God – in the image and likeness of the fallen nature of Adam (Genesis 6:5-6, Galatians 5:19-21, 2 Timothy 3:1-5).

Part 1 of 4

In Part 1 of our chart, God created Adam and Eve on the top line, in His image, according to His likeness. And He commanded them not to eat fruit from the tree of the knowledge of good and evil. The consequence of eating the fruit was death. It came about in time that the serpent (the devil, Satan) deceived Eve into eating the forbidden fruit and she gave it to Adam who also ate. Immediately after they violated God's order, they began their fall into death on the bottom line. That is, immediately after they sinned, they were changed as evidenced by Genesis 2:25 in contrast to 3:4-11. Because of their disobedience, they acquired a fallen, sinful nature. They were no longer the full image and likeness of God.

Take note of the cross. Jesus, God's Christ (God's Messiah), has come and paid the price only He could pay for my sins, your sins, and the sins of the whole world, and to offer me, and you, and the whole world, the gifts of forgiveness of sins, His righteousness, and eternal life with God, the believers' Father (1 John 2:1-3, 23, 25, 3:1-2). At the cross, and subsequently, many men and many women have decided to accept Christ's gifts and have become saints, i.e., righteous or set apart ones, and have gained eternal life. They are coming out of their disobedience, also referred to in the Bible as "darkness". They are destined for the top line, which is referred to in the Bible as "light", because they have chosen to trust and obey the message of Jesus, the Son of God (John 1:1-5, 11-14, 18, 5:24). They are the church, saints set apart to glorify God and to proclaim the gospel (the good news) of His grace – the forgiveness of sin and eternal life. Eventually, all those who are believers will be on the top line where Adam and Eve were created (and where Jesus was born), and have the image, likeness and righteousness of God and His Son, to live forever on the top line with God and His Christ (God's Messiah). But those who have chosen not to trust and obey the message of Jesus shall remain forever in darkness on the bottom line to suffer the eternal wrath of God (John 3:17-20).

Part 2 of 4

In Part 2, the beginning of our story includes the birth of the third child of Adam and Eve (the order mentioned in the Bible), whom they named Seth. At the time of their sin, Adam and Eve had no children. Therefore, every child born of them and all their descendants were born in the fallen state of Adam and Eve. We know this because Genesis 5:1-3 emphasizes to us that Seth was born in the image and likeness of Adam. In the very beginning, it is likely that some descendants of Adam and Eve (such as Seth) were born in between the top line and the bottom line. That is some were born with top line characteristics dominating while others were born with bottom line characteristics dominating. In Genesis chapter 4, it is plausible that Cain and/or Abel were born between the top and bottom lines, and perhaps other siblings, who are not named, were also. For the Bible declares the deeds of

Cain were evil and those of Abel, his brother, were righteous (1 John 3:11-12). In time, however, all mankind ended up on, or was born on, the bottom line (Genesis 6:5-8, Ephesians 2:1-3). That is why the Bible can say essentially, all were born in sin and shaped in iniquity – i.e., ungodliness (Psalm 51:5).

Following Seth, our chart includes Israel. In Exodus chapter 19, God negotiates a covenant with the descendants of Israel saying, "if you will indeed obey My voice and keep My covenant, then you shall be My own possession among all the peoples" (v5). "And you shall be to Me a kingdom of priests and a holy nation" (v6). "And all the people answered together and said, 'All that the Lord has spoken, we will do!'" (v8). God set apart (sanctified) Israel for His purpose.

As we read the book of Joshua, we see that the people kept their covenant commitment to God (top line actions). But after the death of Joshua's generation, we read in the book of the Judges that Israel gradually got away from following after God (Judges 2:6-15). Those who came after Joshua's generation failed to follow God's commandment in Deuteronomy 6:4-15. And so Israel, the people of God, eventually returned to the bottom line as well, just like the rest of mankind, as the book of Jeremiah passionately testifies. At the coming of Jesus, in the New Testament, indicated by the cross in our chart, Israel's leaders were operating (and abiding) on the bottom line. Therefore, they refused to accept the message of God's Messiah (John 8:37-47). Consequently, God has rejected Israel for a time and has turned His attention to saving the Gentiles (i.e., the rest of mankind) primarily through the ministries emanating from the apostles –

Matthew, Peter, Paul, and John, plus Luke – and the church.

Part 3 of 4

In Part 3, we observe that the Bible labels the period before the cross as the Old Testament or Old Covenant – all the books before Matthew. The period from the cross onward, the Bible labels as the New Testament or New Covenant. It includes the books from Matthew through Revelation. When the Bible uses the term "life", especially in the New Testament, it oftentimes is referring to life on the top line. The Bible frequently refers to the bottom line as the "world" or the world system, and "death". The chart emphasizes one profound thought – mankind and Israel (the people of God), both thought to be in the original created-image of Adam, are in fact in the image of fallen Adam (Romans 3:9-18). In this "darkness" (i.e., death), the only light shines from the cross of Christ through the church – the set apart ones of God – who carry both the image of God (what the New Testament calls "the new self" or "new man") and the image of fallen Adam (which the New Testament calls "the old self" or "old man"). Recall that Adam and Eve acquired a fallen sinful nature because of their disobedience and so did their descendants (Ephesians 2:1-3, 4:17-24).

For a brief discussion of man, the image of God, and the sin nature, see Anthropology & Hamartiology: Man and Sin by Greg Herrick.

Let us review our story up to this point. The top line represents the image and likeness of God with Kingdom values, godly character, godly desires and godly obedience. God created

Adam and Eve on the top line. The bottom line represents the fallen nature of Adam that is the opposite of God – unrighteousness, disobedience to the Word of God, worldly values, selfish and fleshly (fallen nature) desires. Because of the sin, all mankind ended up on the bottom line, including Adam and Eve. On the bottom line, I want to give this flesh what this flesh desires, what it thirsts for; what I lust after through my eyes, what I feel and lust for with my hands and my emotions, and what my spirit seeks after. I expect my flesh to have all it desires. And the vast majority of the time, it is all contrary to the character and the will of God. The sin of Adam brought death to all mankind. The sacrifice of Jesus, God's Christ, brought eternal life to those who are willing to believe in His person and message (Romans 5:12-19). Therefore, the Bible is also about death (the bottom line) and life (the top line). The Old Testament paints for us a picture of death. The New Testament points us to life in the midst of what is utter death (when we observe it through God's eyes).

For a more in-depth discussion of evil desires and thoughts, see the article, Where do evil desires and thoughts that arise in a Christian's mind and heart come from? by Dr. Ron Jones.

Part 4 of 4

In Part 4, we conclude the story with the major end time events. Most of us have heard of the second coming of Christ. Prior to actually setting foot on the earth, Jesus will return in the sky to rapture (snatch up) the church to Himself (1 Thessalonians 4:13-17). And so, the church will forever be with Jesus and the Father in an intimate love "relationship" similar to a joyful marriage. After a seven year tribulation period (not shown in the chart), Jesus will return to rule the whole earth from the throne of David (king of Israel) for 1,000 years (the Millennium reign of Christ) when Israel will return to God to join the church in its love "relationship" with the Father and His Son.

During the 1,000-year period (the Millennium), Satan is bound. After 1,000 years, God releases Satan for a time before he is thrown into the lake of fire (his eternal home) along with his demons – fallen angels. Jesus will assemble the whole earth at the Great White Throne Judgment to pass judgment on all unbelievers whom He will cast into the lake of fire along with Satan, for eternity (Matthew 25:31-46, Revelation 20:1-15).

For an in-depth discussion of end time theology and events, see the article, End Times: How is God Going to End All This? by Greg Herrick. Within this article, access the detailed discussion by clicking the article link titled, Survey of Bible Doctrine: The Future. Then return to the main article and scroll down to choose the second article link titled, The Reign of Christ and the Great White Throne (20:1-15).

For an insightful and comprehensive synthesis of the Bible, see the article, The Story And Message of the Bible: What Is It About at understandingthebible.org. Click the "Back to the Top" link at the bottom to enter the site and explore all of its resources.

In Summary

So! The Bible is telling us, then, the story of mankind and the world system through God's eyes. God created Adam and Eve on the top line, without sin, but with freedom of choice. Before they had children, they chose to disobey God. The LORD had previously said to them, "From the tree of the knowledge of good and evil you shall not eat, for in the day that you eat from it you shall surely die" (Genesis 2:17). That is, they would end up on the bottom line. Rebelliously, they ate. Therefore, they ended up on the bottom line in the will and desires of the devil (Satan), separated from God. On the bottom line is where, with a few possible early exceptions, all their descendants were born, including you and me. God, in due time, sent His sinless Son in the form and likeness of a man. He was put to death on a cross – His vicarious sacrifice for the propitiation of the sins of all mankind, because no other man could ever qualify (1 John 2:2, Romans 3:9-12).

The justice of God required that an unblemished, sinless man be sacrificed to pay for sin. No one born from the seed of Adam could ever qualify. But "God so loved the world, that He gave His only begotten Son, that whoever believes in Him should not perish, but have eternal life. For God did not send the Son into the world to judge the world, but that the world should be saved through Him" (John 3:16-17). So our compassionate Father provided us His own sinless Son, born of a woman. In dying for us, Jesus died for all our sins – past, present, and future – except for two. All God requires of us is that we confess Jesus is Lord; and we believe in our heart that Jesus is the Son of God Whom the Father has raised from the dead. When we do, we receive a new nature, a righteous nature, what the Bible calls the new man, yet not replacing the old. We also receive the gift of eternal life with Jesus and with the Father. To help us in the here and now, Jesus has also provided us a Helper in the person of the Holy Spirit to fill us, to teach us, to guide us, and to protect us. In the end, those who believe will be fully conformed to the image and likeness of Jesus Christ (i.e., the image of God) (Genesis 1:26-27, Romans 8:29); and will live in an intimate love "relationship" with Him forever, on the top line, upon Jesus' return to the earth (the second coming). He is coming back! Will you be ready?

Any Questions?

Take some time now to write down your questions as well as document the answers you have already found. Also make notes on your thoughts up to this point.

You may be asking the question, "What did Adam and Eve have to do to get back to the top line?" I am glad you asked that question!

Have you ever thought about how the Bible says many people are not going to be saved because they failed to believe Jesus and to repent of their sins? Now, you may know that we have the doctrine of original sin (the sin nature inherited from Adam) and our own personal sins. And you say to yourself, "Why should God hold me responsible for original sin? I didn't have anything to do with that."

For a broader discussion of original sin, refer to the Bible.org article, Is there original sin, meaning men are sinners because of an inherited' sinful nature passed on by Adam? For a deeper discussion on sin, consider the article, The Doctrine of Sin by Lehman Strauss. Google the previous name at bible.org for a list of other articles by the same author.

When we look at Genesis chapters 2 and 3, what was the basic issue there for Adam and Eve? You see, God said to Adam, of the fruit in the garden you may freely eat of them all but the one – the tree of the knowledge of good and evil. When the serpent (i.e., Satan) came in to deceive Eve, he said, has God told you not to eat of any tree? Eve responded that He said don't eat of this one tree and don't even touch it. For in the day we eat of it, we shall surely die. And what did the serpent say? You won't die. For sure you won't die. This is the real deal: God does not want you to know what He knows. God knows that when you eat of this fruit, you will be like Him, knowing good and evil. That's why He told you not to eat of it. Now, Adam and Eve have a dilemma. God said don't eat of it and here is the reason why you must not eat it. The serpent said, do not believe God. You're going to gain from this. God just does not want you to share in this blessing. Now, Adam and Eve must decide which one they will believe. Will they believe God or will they believe the serpent (Satan)? They chose to act on what the serpent said. And in spite of the revealed consequences, today, most of mankind is doing the same thing when they reject the Bible's Gospel message.

At the right time, mankind having fallen into utter sin, God said, OK, there is a serious problem in that all mankind is born with a sin nature and they're going to do wrong continuously. We know that. Furthermore, there will never be a man born of Adam who can satisfy the penalty for their sins. So what am I going to do? I am going to sacrifice My own sinless Son to pay for all their sins. Up until I truly understood this, my question to God had been, "Why should I be responsible for what Adam and Eve did in the Garden? I didn't have anything to do with that! Plus, through no fault of my own, I now have a sin nature, which Adam and Eve did not have at the time of their sin. Therefore, from birth, my inclination is to sin. If I sin, I can't help myself. So why should I be responsible?"

Therefore, Jesus came to say, if you believe Me and act on that belief, you're not held responsible. I have paid for all you have done and will do. That is why, in the New Testament, it says those who believe in Jesus are not judged. Those who do not believe are judged (doomed) already (John 3:18).

The big question presented to Adam and Eve was, "Do you believe the serpent (Satan) or do you believe God?" Now, today, we all are in the same quandary as Adam and Eve. We look at Adam and Eve and say how could they even make that decision to disobey God? But most of us are making that very same decision today. We are presented with the same dilemma – are we going to believe Jesus (God) or are we going to believe Satan (the devil)? We were born and we live in the midst of Satan's lie. But we think this world system, with its deep philosophies and higher knowledge, is the truth. Jesus has presented us with God's truth. Therefore, in order for mankind to get to the top line, we must believe Jesus, the visible Son of the invisible God, just like Adam and Eve should have believed God the Father in the Garden of Eden. Until Jesus, Adam and Eve, and all their descendants, had no way to get to the top line. For an expansive discussion, see the article, The Judgments - (Past, Present, and Future) by J. Hampton Keathley, III.

Please document your remaining questions and answers and observations, now.

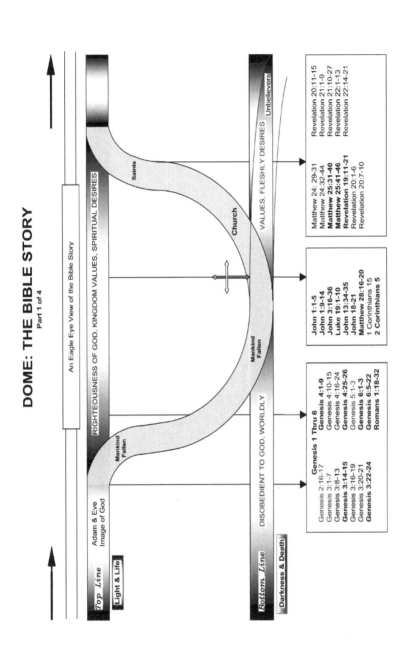

DOME: THE BIBLE STORY
Part 1 of 4

An Eagle Eye View of the Bible Story

Top Line — Adam & Eve Image of God

Light & Life

RIGHTEOUSNESS OF GOD, KINGDOM VALUES, SPIRITUAL DESIRES

Saints

Church

Mankind Fallen

Mankind Fallen

Bottom Line — DISOBEDIENT TO GOD, WORLDLY

VALUES, FLESHLY DESIRES   Unbelievers

Darkness & Death

Genesis 1 Thru 6
Genesis 2:16-17   **Genesis 4:1-9**
Genesis 3:1-7   Genesis 4:10-15
Genesis 3:8-13   Genesis 4:16-24
Genesis 3:14-15   **Genesis 4:25-26**
Genesis 3:16-19   Genesis 5:1-3
Genesis 3:20-21   **Genesis 6:1-3**
Genesis 3:22-24   **Genesis 6:5-22**
                    Romans 1:18-32

John 1:1-5
John 1:9-14
John 3:16-36
Luke 19:1-10
John 13:34-35
John 18-21
Matthew 28:16-20
1 Corinthians 15
2 Corinthians 5

Matthew 24: 29-31
Matthew 24:32-44
Matthew 25:31-40
Matthew 25:41-46
Revelation 19:11-21
Revelation 20:1-6
Revelation 20:7-10

Revelation 20:11-15
Revelation 21:1-9
Revelation 21:10-27
Revelation 22:1-13
Revelation 22:14-21

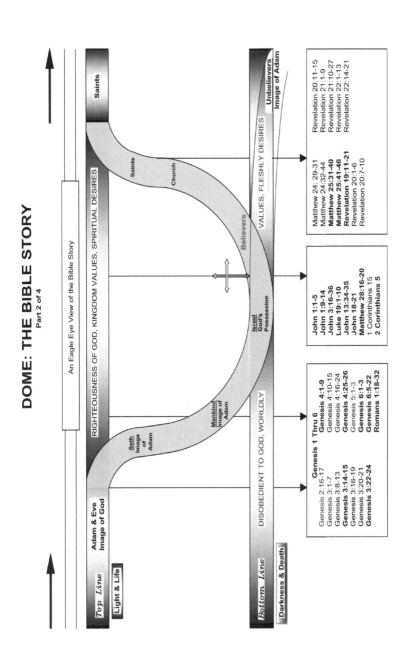

DOME: THE BIBLE STORY
Part 2 of 4

An Eagle Eye View of the Bible Story

Top Line — Light & Life

Saints

RIGHTEOUSNESS OF GOD, KINGDOM VALUES, SPIRITUAL DESIRES

Adam & Eve Image of God

Seth Image of Adam

Mankind Image of Adam

Saints

Church

Believers

Israel God's Possession

Unbelievers — Image of Adam

VALUES, FLESHLY DESIRES

Bottom Line — Darkness & Death

DISOBEDIENT TO GOD, WORLDLY

Genesis 1 Thru 6
Genesis 2:16-17
Genesis 3:1-7
Genesis 3:8-13
Genesis 3:14-15
Genesis 3:16-19
Genesis 3:20-21
Genesis 3:22-24
Genesis 4:1-9
Genesis 4:10-15
Genesis 4:16-24
Genesis 4:25-26
Genesis 5:1-3
Genesis 6:1-3
Genesis 6:5-22
Romans 1:18-32

John 1:1-5
John 1:9-14
John 3:16-36
Luke 19:1-10
John 13:34-35
John 18-21
Matthew 28:16-20
1 Corinthians 15
2 Corinthians 5

Matthew 24: 29-31
Matthew 24:32-44
Matthew 25:31-40
Matthew 25:41-46
Revelation 19:11-21
Revelation 20:1-6
Revelation 20:7-10

Revelation 20:11-15
Revelation 21:1-9
Revelation 21:10-27
Revelation 22:1-13
Revelation 22:14-21

An adaptation of the Top Line / Bottom Line concept of Dr. Charles Baylis, Dallas Theological Seminary.

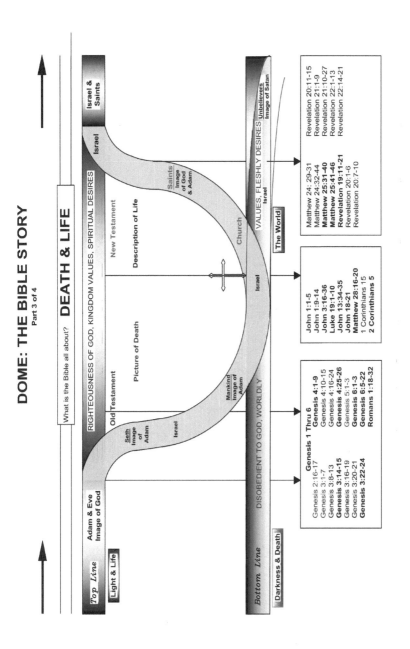

DOME: THE BIBLE STORY
Part 3 of 4

What is the Bible all about? **DEATH & LIFE**

Top Line — *Light & Life*

Adam & Eve Image of God — Israel & Saints

RIGHTEOUSNESS OF GOD, KINGDOM VALUES, SPIRITUAL DESIRES

Old Testament — New Testament

Picture of Death — Description of Life

Seth Image of Adam — Israel — Mankind Image of Adam — Israel — Church — Saints Image of God & Adam — Israel

Bottom Line — *Darkness & Death*

DISOBEDIENT TO GOD, WORLDLY — VALUES, FLESHLY DESIRES Unbelievers Image of Satan

The World

Genesis 1 Thru 6
Genesis 2:16-17
Genesis 3:1-7
Genesis 3:8-13
Genesis 3:14-15
Genesis 3:16-19
Genesis 3:20-21
Genesis 3:22-24
Genesis 4:1-9
Genesis 4:10-15
Genesis 4:16-24
Genesis 4:25-26
Genesis 5:1-3
Genesis 6:1-3
Genesis 6:5-22
Romans 1:18-32

John 1:1-5
John 1:9-14
John 3:16-36
Luke 19:1-10
John 13:34-35
John 18-21
Matthew 28:16-20
1 Corinthians 15
2 Corinthians 5

Matthew 24: 29-31
Matthew 24:32-44
Matthew 25:31-40
Matthew 25:41-46
Revelation 19:11-21
Revelation 20:1-6
Revelation 20:7-10
Revelation 20:11-15
Revelation 21:1-9
Revelation 21:10-27
Revelation 22:1-13
Revelation 22:14-21

An adaptation of the 'Top Line / Bottom Line' concept of Dr. Charles Baylis, Dallas Theological Seminary.

121

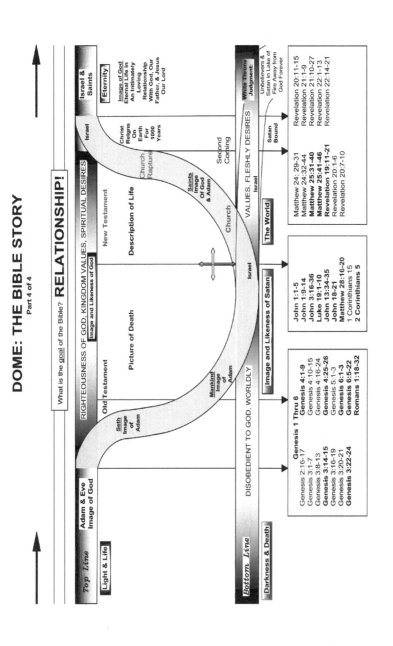

DOME: THE BIBLE STORY
Part 4 of 4

What is the goal of the Bible? **RELATIONSHIP!**

RIGHTEOUSNESS OF GOD, KINGDOM VALUES, SPIRITUAL DESIRES
Image and Likeness of God

VALUES, FLESHLY DESIRES

DISOBEDIENT TO GOD, WORLDLY
Image and Likeness of Satan

Top Line — Light & Life

Adam & Eve — Image of God

Bottom Line — Darkness & Death

Old Testament — Picture of Death

New Testament — Description of Life

Seth Image of Adam

Mankind Image of Adam

Saints Image Of God & Adam

Israel

Church

Israel

Church Rapture

Christ Reigns On Earth For 1000 Years

Second Coming

Satan Bound

Israel & Saints

Eternity:
Image of God Eternal Life in An Intimately Loving Relationship With God, Our Father, & Jesus Our Lord

White Throne Judgment:
Unbelievers & Satan in Lake of Fire Away from God Forever

Israel

The World

Genesis 2:16-17	**Genesis 1 Thru 6**
Genesis 3:1-7	Genesis 4:1-9
Genesis 3:8-13	Genesis 4:10-15
Genesis 3:14-15	Genesis 4:16-24
Genesis 3:16-19	**Genesis 4:25-26**
Genesis 3:20-21	Genesis 5:1-3
Genesis 3:22-24	**Genesis 6:1-3**
	Genesis 6:5-22
	Romans 1:18-32

John 1:1-5
John 1:9-14
John 3:16-36
Luke 19:1-10
John 13:34-35
John 18-21
Matthew 28:16-20
1 Corinthians 15
2 Corinthians 5

Matthew 24: 29-31
Matthew 24:32-44
Matthew 25:31-40
Matthew 25:41-46
Revelation 19:11-21
Revelation 20:1-6
Revelation 20:7-10

Revelation 20:11-15
Revelation 21:1-9
Revelation 21:10-27
Revelation 22:1-13
Revelation 22:14-21

The Will Of God

As we read and study the Scriptures, we should always keep in mind that Scripture clarifies and expounds on Scripture. This is the truth behind the "related text" concept discussed in chapter 4. In this chapter, we are focused on obtaining an understanding of "related text" and how it can help us grasp a broader and coherent comprehension of the Scriptures. Our subject is the will of God. Please pay particular attention to how the referenced Scriptures inform, integrate into and expound on the biblical concepts in our narrative.

The Wickedness of Man

"Then the Lord saw that the wickedness of man was great on the earth, and that every intent of the thoughts of his heart was only evil continually. And the Lord was sorry that He had made man on the earth, and He was grieved in His heart" (Genesis 6:5-6).

"The heart is more deceitful than all else And is desperately sick; Who can understand it?" (Jeremiah 17:9).

Let us revisit the Bible story by first taking a look at Genesis 2:16-17 and second, a look at Genesis 6:5-6. In Genesis 2:16-17, God commands Adam not to eat of the tree of the knowledge of good and evil. That was the only constraint. And it came with an explicit consequence – death! What was the will of God for Adam, and by implication, Eve and all their offspring as well? Obedience! In Genesis 6:5-6, we are told that all mankind has become corrupt, consumed with evil thoughts and intentions, continually. Further, we are told that God "was grieved in His heart" that He had made man. Why was God's heart suffering so much grief? Because man had disobeyed God and eaten of the forbidden fruit which resulted in man losing his "relationship" with God and propagating evil. Consequently, man's wickedness as described in Genesis 6:5 was extremely evil and growing! If Adam and Eve, alone with all their descendants, had obeyed that one commandment of God, we would never have known the picture painted by Genesis 6:5-6 and Jeremiah 17:9, and the continuing consequence thereof even to the current day.

"Now the earth was corrupt in the sight of God, and the earth was filled with violence" (Genesis 6:11). As a consequence of Adam's sin, there was (and still is) no peace on the earth. Hostility ruled the day. What was God to do? God decided He would destroy all flesh except for a remnant composed of Noah, his family, and the animals. The instrument He would use would be the great flood of water. However, the great flood did not destroy all evil nor the curse. Therefore, the corruption of mankind continued, perhaps at a slower pace; but it has continued to the present day (Matthew 15:15-20). Why is it so difficult for mankind, then, to obey the will of the Father?

Romans 1:18-32 describes the progression of man's corruption. It also paints a picture of the current state of man – Total Depravity as explained in this article by Steven J. Cole. A depraved mind is one whose thoughts and intentions are reprobate, worthless, disapproved in the eyes of God, and contrary to God's image and likeness (i.e., God's heart, His character). Such is the heart and mind of all mankind in their natural state. Remember, "We were born in sin and shaped in iniquity." Sin is what we know and desire in our natural state. For an in-depth discussion on the matter, see the article, Condemnation, or, the Universal Need of Righteousness by Allen Ross.

Into this reality stepped Jesus, the Son of God, to teach us the truth of who we are in comparison to who God is. Without God, we would have no idea what righteousness actually looks like. Therefore, God the Father sent His Son, in the visible form of man, to educate and enlighten us in truth; and to teach us to live our lives according to God's standards and not according to the standards of society (what the Bible calls "the world" or "world system"). But there are precious few who even desire a holy life or even know what one is. Why?

Genesis 1:26-27 informs us that, from the beginning, God's

plan for man was for us to be in the image and likeness of God, i.e., his behavior was to be as God's behavior. The intentions of his heart were to be the same as God's heart. That plan has not changed. When we look at the New Testament, we are told that Jesus is the Son (John 1:34) and image (Colossians 1:15) of the invisible God. Jesus tells us in John 8:29 that the Father is with Him because "I always do the things that are pleasing to Him". Jesus is always obedient to the Father. In John 14:31, again Jesus tells us "as the Father gave Me commandment, even so I do". One of the things Jesus is attempting to get the people of His day (and us) to see is that He is what God originally intended for all mankind to be (minus His deity, of course). When we consider the degenerated state of man as compared to what God's original intent was, what is the will of God for us in our sin-sick and evil state?

The Will of God

"What is the will of God?" "What is the will of God for my life?" Probably every individual who has ever lived has asked one of these questions at some point in their lives, including the vast majority of those who claim there is no God. Many books have been written concerning the subject – some large and some small. However, I believe the universal will of God for every individual who has been or will be born can be expressed in a single word – **Obedience**! That's too simple, huh? Don't be too quick to draw your conclusion.

In Ephesians 4:11-13, the Bible tells us that Christians are to attain to "a mature man, to the measure of the stature which belongs to the fullness of Christ". Jesus is clear in His understanding that the will of the Father for Him is **Obedience**. And we are to strive to attain to the stature of Jesus. Therefore, we should be the same as Jesus in our understanding that the will of the Father for us is "Obedience!" Otherwise, we are destined to do evil continually in the sight of the Lord. Without Jesus, it is our very nature to do evil contrary to God's nature and commandments.

What about the non-Christian? What is the will of God for his or her life? The same as that for the Christian – Learn, Believe, Trust, and then Obey! You are to believe the Gospel (the good news) of Jesus Christ Who says, "I am the way, and the truth, and the life; no one comes to the Father, but through Me" (John 14:6). "If you confess with your mouth Jesus as Lord, and believe in your heart that God raised Him from the dead, you shall be saved; for with the heart, man believes, resulting in righteousness, and with the mouth, he confesses, resulting in salvation" (Romans 10:9-10). Simply put, the will of God for the non-Christian is to learn, believe, trust, and obey God! For the Lord God "is patient toward you, not wishing for any to perish but for all to come to repentance" (2 Peter 3:9). Even now, His out-stretched hand is waiting on you to call on Him and repent.

Scriptures teach us that when we accept Jesus as the One who can save us from the penalty of our sins, we are a new creation (2 Corinthians 5:17). We receive a new nature to counteract the old. And these two natures are constantly battling for superiority over our heart, mind and our flesh (Galatians 5:16-26, Romans 7:14-25). If we are to have any chance of getting to and remaining substantially in obedience, we must confront three primary obstacles or hurdles: *willingness*, *humility*, and *submission*.

Willingness

This is the first and foremost hurdle. Several years ago, I was having a serious struggle with obeying God in a particular area (unfortunately, I cannot recall the details). And the devil was having a field day with me because of my failure until finally, I decided to have a more serious conversation with God about it. I needed answers. After much wrestling with the issue, one of the questions I asked God was, "Why can't I be obedient in this particular matter? Why am I having such a struggle with this?" And He said to me, "You are not willing." What! I knew I was willing! That was a foregone conclusion as far as I was concerned. I was fully committed to God in all things. How could God say such a thing? So now, my struggle began all over again. I was in agreement with the goal. I wanted my behavior to conform. So what was my problem? Over the next several days, God revealed to me that my willingness was a half-hearted willingness; and so was my commitment to it. I had set unspoken limits on how far I was willing to go. I was reluctant to sacrifice everything that was necessary.

To help you grasp this concept more fully, consider this. The Bible states very clearly and emphatically in Ephesians 5:22, "Wives, be subject to your own husbands, as to the Lord. For the husband is the head of the wife, as Christ also is the head of the church". The King James Version uses the word "submit" in place of "be subject to". In 1 Peter 3:4-6, we see Sarah, Abraham's wife, lifted up as our example for today as we read that "Sarah obeyed Abraham, calling him lord". Finally, a very telling passage is found in Ephesians 5:33, "and let the wife see to it that she respects her husband". How many wives can quote these passages, claim to be submissive and respectful, but in fact are doing so only when it pleases them; when it makes them feel good or look good in their own eyes? What about all the other times? What about behind closed doors? What is the percentage of wives that you know who say they are submissive; but who are truly willing to be subordinate and respectful to their husbands in the manner of Sarah? The answer in actuality is likely a very few. Why?

For an informative perspective on the subject of wives submitting to their own husbands, see the article The Submission of The Christian Wife by Bob Deffinbaugh, which also provides a biblical perspective of submission for all Christians.

And men, Scripture commands us as well in Ephesians 5:25-33, "Husbands, love your wives, just as Christ also loved the church and gave Himself up [sacrificed Himself] for her..." So Husbands ought also to love their own wives as their own bodies." How many husbands loudly proclaim their love for their wives? But how many actually love their own wife enough to sacrifice himself for her in all things? Maybe in a life or death situation, yes; but what about everyday mundane interactions? I must confess I am still struggling. And why? Because I am not yet actually willing to make the sacrifice to die to myself as Jesus did. I am struggling to get totally passed the obstacle of willingness in this area, mostly because of pride and selfishness.

For a more in-depth perspective on the subject of willingness, see the article, <u>Abraham, The Man Willing to Make The Ultimate Sacrifice</u> by Crickett Keeth.

Humility

"I can't stop thinking about me" is an anxious phrase I learned from my wife who heard it from God. It seems to sum up the problem with most of us when it comes to the hurdle of humility. Consider carefully the times you were wounded by the insensitivity of a family member or friend. Should you confront them about it, in many instances, they would truly be surprised at your complaint. How could that be? Don't they know they are hurting you? You see, in most instances, people are not hurting us intentionally. They are simply getting what they want while being oblivious to its impact on others. No one has to teach us to look out for number one. We are all struggling to be looked upon as "being somebody" to look up to. In teaching our children key relationship concepts, humility has to be up near the top in difficulty. Can you recall your first attempts at teaching your child the concept of humility in the midst of company? I can hear their initial response ringing in my ears even now, a response I had not anticipated – "Why?" Therefore, I did not have a response that made sense to him at that moment.

I get that same uneasy feeling when I read Paul's instructions to the <u>Philippians in 2:3-16</u>. "Do nothing from selfishness or empty conceit, but with *humility* of mind let each of you regard one another as more important than himself; do not merely look out for your own personal interests, but also for the interests of

132

others" [Italics mine]. Paul continues by asking the Philippians to see Christ as their example Who humbled Himself to the Father "to the point of death, even death on a cross" (v 8). His humility led Him to obey His Father's will even unto death. But for the rest of us, it is a difficult thing to choose to humble ourselves to others, and even to God. Yet God commands us to follow in the footsteps of Jesus, our Lord and Savior. We must realize God created us for His good pleasure, not the other way around. We are the sheep of His pasture not the shepherd of our own lives. Until we consider God infinitely more important than self and His wisdom infinitely higher than our own, it will be impossible to humble ourselves consistently before Him. In other words, we tend to think more highly of ourselves than we ought to think (Romans 12:3) leaving little room for the grace of God to work in our lives.

For a broader discussion on the subject of humility, see the article, Humility by Kenneth Boa.

Prayer: Father, we confess to You that we have failed to humble ourselves before You and before our fellow man. Cleanse us. Erase the pride and self-centeredness from our hearts. Make us more like Your Son, Jesus, for "I can't stop thinking about me!" Amen.

Submission

Here we focus our attention on the failure of man to yield himself or herself to the will, plans, and purposes of the Almighty, living God Who created us. Submission means to put oneself under another, to be subject to the authority of another, to be in obedience under another. <u>Isaiah 14:12-15</u> paints a vivid picture of one who believes he must submit to no one, not even to God! Instead of submitting to God, his plan is to become like God. I am always astonished at the many people who say things like, "God has a lot of explaining to do". Or, "God has a lot to answer for". Such an attitude points to a recalcitrant heart, in the ultimate sense. They seem to be confused about Who is the Creator and who is the creature. They have forgotten or have never known Who is all-powerful and who is powerless. From toddler through adulthood, we resist the thought of submission. We want to be god of our own lives. We want to do things our own way, in the irreverent and disrespectful manner of Adam and Eve, in spite of what God has said. We want the glory for anything we do or can claim we did. But our Creator makes it plain throughout the Bible that we must subordinate what we desire to His sovereignty, totally, in the fear of the Lord. Until we accept the fact that God will always have the last say in any matter, and we cannot overcome that, we will not be totally submissive to Him.

So the question is, "Are **you** willing to humble **yourself** before God and His people (forsaking your pride), and to submit yourself to God's will and His way, for your own good?" Why not take a moment (or a day if necessary) to ponder seriously the implications of this question and your response to it.

Now, what is your answer? Record your thoughts in detail in your notes along with the date, time, and place.

We Are Children of God

God is all about relationship. "God is love" (1 John 4:8). He

134

knows exactly the kind of relationship He is looking for in His people – His sons and His daughters. He is "the God of gods and the Lord of lords, the great, the mighty, and the awesome God" (Deuteronomy 10:17). We were created by Him and for Him. We did not create ourselves. Therefore, He has the right to demand whatever He wants from us and for us. And everything He desires of us originates from His vast, unfailing, unconditional love for us. Recall that the book of Deuteronomy is the "Book of Relationship". That is, it describes in detail how the children of God (in these latter years, children include those who have accepted or received Jesus Christ as savior) are to interact with the Father and He with them. Deuteronomy 10:12-13 lays out the fundamental requirements for the type of personal relationship our heavenly Father yearns to have with His children. That is, it points out the key responsibilities of the children toward the Father. It is about what He wants from the relationship or what we must bring to an intimate relationship with Him. OK! I hear you right now. You want to know, "What's in it for me? What do I get out of it?" Before we answer that, take a moment to revisit "Humility" and meditate on how "I can't stop thinking about me."

In return, you get God's everlasting lovingkindness and God's loving favor – "Yet on your fathers did the Lord set His affection [or loving favor] to love them, and He chose their descendants [seed] after them, even you above all peoples, as it is this day" (Deuteronomy 10:15).

The foundational requirements of Deuteronomy 10:12-13 are not meant just for Israel but also for anyone who believes in Jesus today (Galatians 3:26-29). So let us turn our attention to the message of Deuteronomy 10:12-13:

"And now, Israel, what does the Lord your God require from you, but to *fear* the Lord your God, to *walk* in all His ways and *love* Him, and to *serve* the Lord your God with all your heart and with all your soul, and to *keep the Lord's commandments* and *His statutes* which I am commanding you today *for your good?*" [Italics mine].

As we dissect this passage, from God's perspective, we find the following keys to a right relationship with the Father Who saves sinners from the wrath of God:

Fear or Reverence: Includes the following meaning – honor, profound awe and respect, esteem, pleasing behavior. He is holy! A holy God is to be revered, regarded as worthy of great honor with awed respect and fear, and "an overwhelming feeling of wonder and admiration". It "presupposes an intrinsic merit and inviolability in the one honored and a similar depth of feeling in the one [doing] the honoring" (Merriam-Webster Dictionary.com). He is the one worthy of the highest respect, all glory, all praise.

I grew up in a household where my dad tolerated absolutely no disrespect toward him or my mother. When disobedience, arrogance, or pride, raised its ugly, sinful head, he stamped it out immediately just like God the Father in the Old Testament. Therefore, I had a "healthy fear" of and respect for my dad. How much more should I fear, honor, respect and esteem our loving, great, mighty and awesome God? Reference Hebrews 12:4-11, 18-29 for scriptural clarity.

Walk: Nine times in Deuteronomy, Moses admonishes the Israelites to walk (i.e., live) in all the ways of God. The New Testament teaches the same (John 14:21-24). As Christians, we are in the world but not of the world (society at large). Our citizenship is in heaven. Therefore, we are to walk (i.e., live) like heavenly citizens instead of like citizens of the world (society at large). We are called to a higher standard so that the rest of society may see us as being set apart from them, and holy unto God. God calls Christians to be a peculiar people, to be light in this world of darkness so that the unbeliever might notice our light and yearn for a better way; and then come to the Light. Obedience to this principle requires a submissive behavior born of a humble submission to God. The prerequisite of such a walk is willingness, humility, submission, and total trust in Jesus Christ. Trust is reliance on the character, ability, strength, and truth of Jesus Christ, otherwise (or commonly) referred to as *faith*. "Therefore, we are confident that God is Who He says He is and God will do what He says He will do." In everything, we should live (i.e., walk) to please God and passionately desire to be like His Son. Why not make this your daily prayer?

Love: In the biblical sense, love goes beyond feelings to a decision of the will. Therefore, we actively manifest biblical love in the things we do rather than the things we say. It also includes an emotional component as in Deuteronomy 10:20-21, "You shall fear the Lord your God; you shall *serve* Him and *cling* to Him." "He is your *praise* and He is *your God*..." [Italics mine]. This word "cling" means to hold on tightly and to have a strong emotional attachment to, or dependence on God like little children. The word "love" is used sixteen times in Deuteronomy to speak of

God's commitment to love His people and God's command to His people to love Him. Love is important to God, for He Himself is love. In John 14:21, Jesus declares, "He who has My commandments and keeps them, he it is who loves Me; and he who loves Me shall be loved by My Father, and I will love him, and will disclose Myself to him". I call this the love triangle – Father, Son, and believer. When asked which is the great commandment in the Law, Jesus quoted Deuteronomy 6:5 saying, "'You shall love the Lord your God with all your heart, and with all your soul, and with all your mind.' This is the great and foremost commandment. The second is like it, 'you shall love your neighbor as yourself'" (Matthew 22:37-38). Loving God and loving who and what He loves is the greatest thing you can do in your Christian walk.

Serve: "*Serve* the Lord your God with *all your heart* and with *all your soul*" (Deuteronomy 10:12) [emphasis added] doesn't leave much room for your desires except your desire to please Him. In the Hebrew, the word translated "serve" means to attend to someone or to wait upon someone as would a slave or servant. In some instances, the same Hebrew word has been translated "minister to". To serve the Lord also means you are to serve others as Jesus did and as He teaches us saying, "whoever wishes to become great among you shall be your servant, and whoever wishes to be first among you shall be your slave; just as the Son of Man [Jesus] did not come to be served, but to serve, and give His life a ransom for many" (Matthew 20:26-28).

Please access the following articles for an extended discussion by other authors: Loving By Serving by Jerry Bridges and

Willingness to Serve on the Bible.org website. See also Full Service Christians in a Self-Service World by Wesley Willis.

Keep: Deuteronomy 10:13 commands Israel "to keep the Lord's commandments and His statutes...for your good". Moses uses the word "keep" in Deuteronomy 27 times; nearly all of them related to keeping the Lord's commandments and statutes. He used the word "obey" 14 times, and the word "observe" 24 times, in the sense of keeping God's commandments, statutes, ordinances and testimonies. In Scripture, statutes express moral and spiritual duties; judgments are measures designed to secure social justice. Testimonies declare the Lords will, and the arm of the Lord on behalf of His people, and His wisdom (Unger's Bible Handbook, 1981, p. 141).

So, at least 50 times in this one book, Moses, God's prophet, pleads with the people of God to "keep every commandment which I am commanding you today". The nature and number of Moses' entreaties are indicative of God's problem with man. It is the nature of man to operate independent of God, usually in ways that are the opposite of God. Here, Moses is warning Israel to set aside their own lusts and desires in favor of what God has commanded. In the New Testament, Jesus says, if you want a relationship with Me, deny yourself. Forsake what you want. Take up what the Lord wants; and that for your own good (Luke 9:23). Simply stated, we are to obey God in all our ways. See the article, The Cross and Christianity (Luke 9:18-26) by Bob Deffinbaugh for an expanded discussion.

In essence, what Moses is telling the people of God in Deuteronomy is, they must have a total commitment to God's way instead of the world's way. "We are no longer under the Law", you say. Yes. But the commitment principle still stands. Jesus fulfilled the Law through His love and obedience, and instituted a new Covenant of Grace that we know as the New Testament, the foundation and pillar of which is love. We are to read it, believe it, and live it. And it too tells us to commit our lives totally to the Lord, Jesus Christ. For Paul says in Romans 12:1-2, "I urge you therefore, brethren, by the mercies of God, to present your bodies a living and holy sacrifice, acceptable to God, which is your spiritual service of worship. And do not be conformed to this world [society at large], but be transformed by the renewing of your mind, that you may prove what the will of God is, that which is good and acceptable and perfect". God wants all of you and everything you have – your heart, your mind, your will, your body, your time, your talents, your possessions, your desires, your affections – to be used in accomplishing His will on earth instead of your will.

Walk As His Children

Through Christians, at the sacrifice of our own significance and glory (Luke 9:23-24), God intends to demonstrate to the world (society at large) what He, the invisible God, is truly like so that the world might come to know Him and accept Him. That means Christians (God's children) must strive constantly to attain "to a mature man [or woman], to the measure of the stature which belongs to the fullness of Christ" (Ephesians 4:13) through our obedience to the teachings of Jesus and His apostles (e.g., see 1 John 3). Amen!

140

The will of God for His children is the same as the will of any loving parent – *obedience*! Consider that we were born knowing how to do wrong but we must be trained to do what is right (Deuteronomy 6:4-9). Our obedience, especially when God's commandments don't sit well with us, makes us participants in and contributors to Christ's ministry of reconciliation. You see, "God was in Christ reconciling the world to Himself, not counting their trespasses [sins] against them, and He has committed to us the word of reconciliation" (2 Corinthians 5:19). That work should be the primary ministry of His followers today. "Therefore be imitators of God, as beloved children; and walk in love [for those in the world], just as Christ also loved you, and gave Himself up for us, an offering and a sacrifice to God as a fragrant aroma" (Ephesians 5:1-2). "This I say therefore, and affirm together with the Lord, that you walk no longer just as the Gentiles [unbelievers] also walk, in the futility of their mind, being darkened in their understanding, excluded from the life of God, because of the ignorance that is in them, because of the hardness of their heart" (Ephesians 4:17-18).

So, if you are not yet one of His children, won't you, please, choose to believe and obey Jesus and take advantage of God's amnesty program today by receiving Jesus as your Savior? Surrender your heart to Him and pray a simple sincere prayer from the heart. Confess the truth that you are a sinner in need of a savior. Surrender yourself totally to Him with a sincere heart. Ask Him to forgive you of your sins and be your Savior and to teach you all that you must know from His Bible. He will do the rest if you speak to Him from a broken spirit with a sincere and contrite heart (Reference Psalm 51).

After you have accepted Christ as your Savior, remember always, your responsibility is to learn of Him, love Him, trust Him, and **obey Him** in accordance with Deuteronomy 10:12-13 and the New Covenant! For this is His will for you, for your good!

7

The Thread Of Disobedience

In our previous chapter, we gained an appreciation for the universal will of God for every human being who has been and will be born. Let us now turn our attention to how the thread of God's universal will plays out in the Bible using the "related text" concept. But before we do, I would like to give you a beautiful way of perceiving Bible threads. It does not come from me but from God Himself. Yesterday, as I worked on this book, my number one grandson stopped by to visit me. We talked about the objective of my book and he related his attempts to read the Bible with understanding. His complaint was that he knew many of the Bible stories. He could get messages from them. But he could not perceive a relationship between or amongst them. Each one seemed to be a separate little island unto itself. As we discussed the concept of Bible threads, God gave me a wonderful way of visualizing these threads and their function.

Have you ever seen clothes hanging on a line? For those who have not, picture a line in the backyard, usually of rope or wire, strung between two or more strong poles five to six feet tall and ten to twelve feet apart. Now picture clothes hanging on that line to dry from the heat of the sun. *As an analogy, picture each piece of clothing as a book of the Bible and the clothesline as a Bible thread.* Now, imagine the books (clothes) are hanging on the Bible thread (clothesline) in the sequence they appear in the Bible. *The Bible thread is what each book has in common with the other.* This is what Christ expects us to observe and note as we study His Word. This is an important concept. So, before you proceed further, please take a moment to get this concept well defined in your mind. Sketch it out on paper if necessary. Record it in your notes.

A Bible thread, then, is the link or bridge that connects the stories and books. A Bible thread is what each story and/or book has in common with other books or stories from Genesis to Revelation. However, in your studies, do not expect a particular thread to be addressed in every book or story. And this series does not address all threads. Only indispensable threads are included to prepare you to read your Bible enthusiastically with great understanding, and to allow you the joy of discovering other threads for yourself through your own daily Bible study.

In this present chapter, the thread that holds everything together is "obedience versus disobedience" (analogous to the clothesline). Now picture all of the individual Bible books as hanging on that thread – "obedience versus disobedience". Therefore, since this is a major thread, we should expect to see the Scriptures addressing obedience or disobedience in nearly every book, certainly within each subdivision in both testaments. So let's see how this thread plays out using the "related text" concept.

Obedience Versus Disobedience

In Genesis chapter 2, our first parents had one commandment to obey. In Genesis chapter 3, Adam and Eve, before they had children, chose to disobey God's single command. That decision plunged all mankind to the bottom line resulting in the whole earth being cursed, even through today.

In Genesis chapter 4, the first-born child arrives in the person of Cain. Shortly thereafter, the second son is born in the person of Abel. Scripture refers to them in terms of the evil and the righteous one, respectively, because of the nature of their sacrifices and their behavior (1 John 3:11-12). God was not satisfied with Cain's sacrifice. So the evil child rose up and murdered the righteous child simply because God had approved Abel's sacrifice and not Cain's. We also see the evil continue in Cain's descendants in Genesis 4.

In Genesis chapter 5, we again see the righteous child in Seth and his descendants, including Noah. Evil deeds persist throughout Genesis (e.g., Genesis 37:12-36) and Exodus although accompanied from time to time by acts of righteousness.

In Leviticus, God establishes the statutes and ordinances for a formal relationship between Him and His people. Leviticus also contains societal rules of human relationships and order according to the culture of God's kingdom. The book closes (chapter 26) with emphasis on the blessings for obedience and the severe penalties for disobedience.

In Numbers, we observe the census, the rebellions, the punishment and the wanderings due to Israel's rebellion. Israel

145

complains and weeps because they want meat instead of manna. Therefore, they longed to be back in Egypt. We also see the children of Israel fearing to go in and take possession of the Promised Land even though Moses and Aaron pleaded with them not to rebel against the Lord and not to fear the inhabitants of the land. Yet they persisted and engendered the anger of God which Moses quells by reminding God of His righteous character: "The Lord is slow to anger and abundant in lovingkindness, forgiving iniquity and transgression; but He will by no means clear the guilty, visiting the iniquity of the fathers on the children to the third and the fourth generations" (14:18). Man's disbelief in and his failure to reverence and trust God is one thing that severely angers God. How can a person not believe and trust the one and only true and living God after seeing His great power and His faithfulness as Israel has? How can such a thing be? Even nature, indeed, all of creation, testifies to His awesome power and His unfathomable creativity and wisdom.

In the book of Deuteronomy, Moses presents the rules for an intimate personal relationship between a personal God, Yahweh (the covenant name of God) and His people. Therefore, repeatedly, Moses commands the children of Israel, "you shall love the Lord Your God with all your heart and with all your soul and with all your might" (6:5). "Then it shall come about, because you listen to these judgments and keep and do them, that the Lord your God will keep with you His covenant and His lovingkindness which He swore to your forefathers" (7:12). In chapters 27, 28, and 30, Moses lays out the blessings for obedience and the curses for disobedience. Throughout the book, Moses is obviously very concerned that the children of Israel will disobey God's covenant.

Therefore, He repeatedly admonishes them to obey God. Obey God!

At this point in the Bible story, then, the covenant – the rules of a formal and a personal relationship with the loving Father and the all knowing God of the universe, Yahweh, is well established and clearly understood. The big question now becomes, "What will be the outcome – obedience or disobedience; blessings or curses?"

In the book of Joshua, having assumed the leadership role from Moses, Joshua leads the children of Israel to conquer the land of Canaan and to do all that Moses had commanded them to do. Joshua and his generation were obedient to the covenant that the people had made with their God. The book closes with a focus on their obedience – "And Israel served the Lord all the days of Joshua and all the days of the elders who survived Joshua, and had known all the deeds of the Lord which He had done for Israel" (24:31). Deuteronomy 6:5-9 tells God's people (including today's Christians) how to prepare and protect the future generations from disobedience in the midst of constant spiritual warfare. Joshua's generation obeyed God.

The book of Judges opens with the disobedience of the people even before announcing the appearance of the angel of the Lord. The author presents a list of places that Israel did not conquer and utterly destroy. Instead, they made a covenant with the inhabitants even though God said, "you shall make no covenant with the inhabitants of this land; you shall tear down their alters. But you have not obeyed Me; what is this you have done?" (2:2). Joshua died. "All that generation also were gathered to their fathers; and there arose another generation after them who did not know the LORD, nor yet the work which He had done for Israel" (Judges 2:10). This generation did not prepare their children for the battle – i.e., the spiritual battle – in accordance with Deuteronomy 6:5-9. Therefore, their children did not know God and his works, nor did they keep God's covenant. And so, they were drawn away from the LORD into disobedience. "Then the sons of Israel did evil in the sight of the LORD and served the Baals, and they forsook the LORD, the God of their gathers" (2:1-12). Time after time and judge after judge, Israel disobeys God. Therefore, to chastise them, God allows the surrounding nations to plunder and enslave them. "And when the sons of Israel cried to the Lord, the Lord raised up a deliverer [a judge] for the sons of Israel to deliver them" (3:9). Judges paints a picture of what happens when God's people disobey Him by mixing with Satan's people. In general, they are drawn away from the true and living God (the God of the Bible) to embrace what is not God, a counterfeit. In order to stress the point of disobedience, the book of Judges closes with these final words: "In those days there was no king in Israel; everyone did what was right in his own eyes" (21:25), instead of what was right in the eyes of God, as the covenant commanded.

The period of the judges is followed by the kings of Israel starting in 1 Samuel and ending in 2 Chronicles. The kings of Israel take up a large portion of the historical period. During this period, after the death of Solomon, the nation of Israel was divided into the Northern Kingdom, Israel, and the Southern Kingdom, Judah. In the details, the Bible's focus is on what is in the heart of each king, whether good or evil, based on his adherence to the covenant with their God. God evaluates each king on his moral character and covenant leadership. More often than not, the Bible declares that the king "did evil in the sight of the Lord" beginning with the very first king of Israel, King Saul. For a chart showing the nature of each king's heart, see, Chart of Israel's and Judah's Kings and Prophets by Craig T. Owens,

In the prophets, the first subheading in the first book, Isaiah, is "Rebellion of God's People". They have turned from doing good in the eyes of the Lord to doing evil. God pleads with them to "Wash yourselves, make yourselves clean; Remove the evil of your deeds from My sight. Cease to do evil, Learn to do good; Seek justice, Reprove the ruthless; Defend the orphan, Plead for the widow" (Isaiah 1:16-17). Throughout the prophets, the reader observes God's pleadings with Israel to return to Him in obedience to their covenant with Him only to see them reject God's pleadings. But God is faithful to His covenant with them, both the blessings and the curses. After much longsuffering, God loses His patience and disperses Israel (the Northern Kingdom) from the Promised Land; and scatters them throughout key cities in the nation of Assyria, leaving only a remnant of the poor and misfits. Nearly a hundred and forty years later, in disgust, God exiled Judah (the Southern Kingdom) to Babylon. Again, it was because of their disobedience. For the details, read the prophet Jeremiah.

God promised restoration and prosperity, in Deuteronomy 30:1-10, if Israel would only "return" to Him with their whole heart. In His grace (divine favor), after seventy years in Babylon, God allows a remnant of the people to return to the Promised Land only to see them fall into their rebellious ways. So God declares that "the great and terrible day of the Lord" is coming after the days of a future Elijah the prophet when He will utterly destroy every evildoer" (Malachi 4:1-5). Therefore, for four hundred years, God stopped speaking to His people until He spoke through His Son, Jesus. And Israel even disobeyed, rejected, and killed God's Son.

As we leave the Old Testament, we see that Israel, a people for God's own possession, is just as unrighteous and evil as the nations around them. The Bible student can well appreciate that the present thread is aptly called "The Thread of Disobedience" instead of "the thread of obedience". The Old Testament rightly declares, "The Lord has looked down from heaven upon the sons of men, To see if there are any who understand, Who seek after God. They have all turned aside; together they have become corrupt; There is no one who does good, not even one" (Psalm 14:2-3). How will man find his way out of this hopeless predicament? In His love and compassion, God has promised a Messiah (a Christ), the King and Liberator of the Jewish people (and all mankind) as in Jeremiah 23:5-6:

> 5 "Behold, the days are coming," declares the LORD, "When I shall raise up for David a righteous Branch; And He will reign as king and act wisely And do justice and righteousness in the land. 6 " In His days Judah will be saved, And Israel will dwell securely; And this is His name by which He will be called, 'The LORD our righteousness.'

Entering the New Testament, we observe that Matthew declares in the very first chapter of the book that Israel, as a consequence of their disobedience, is in need of a savior – "And she [the virgin, Mary] will bear a Son; and you [Joseph] shall call His name Jesus, for it is He Who will save His people from their sins" (1:21). The author of the book of John seems to stress and emphasize the extent of the world's, and Israel's, separation from God due to their disobedience. He declares in the first few verses of the book, "There was the true light [Jesus] which, coming into the world, enlightens every man. He was in the world, and the world was made through Him, and the world did not know Him. He came to His own [Israel], and those who were His own did not receive Him" (1:9-11). What a terrible indictment of all mankind, even those chosen of God as a people for His own possession.

In His ministry, Jesus confronts the disobedience of Israel while emphasizing His own obedience to the Father (John 8). "And He [God] Who sent Me is with Me; He has not left Me alone, [*as He has you*] for I always do the things that are pleasing to Him" (John 8:29) [Brackets mine]. "But that the world may know that *I love the Father*, and as the Father gave Me commandment, even so I do" (John 14:31)(Emphasis mine). Jesus was saying to them in summary, it is My obedience that proves My love for the Father. And it is your disobedience that proves you have no love for the Father (John 14:21-24). (Recall in Deuteronomy the pleadings of Moses to love and obey the Lord). Likewise today, our obedience to the Son proves our love for the Father just as our disobedience proves we too have no love for the Father.

Jesus' actions and teachings are to be understood in the context of the will of God as presented in the Old Testament in contrast to Israel's, and all of mankind's, utter disobedience.

As we see, the Bible paints a woeful picture of our hopeless world fully separated from the Creator. Because of our disobedience, our world is in deep darkness far from the light of God. No one even seeks God on their own. Mankind's disobedience is complete. This Bible thread leads the reader to one inevitable conclusion – without Jesus, there is no hope of escape from the promised wrath of God on this world replete with sorrow, hostility, and sin. The wrath of God rests on every unbeliever, to be revealed in the Day of Judgment, "the great and terrible day of the Lord". That is why Jesus wanted us to know that He alone is the way out. "I am the way, and the truth, and the life; no one comes to the Father, but through Me" (John 14:6). "And there is salvation in no one else; for there is no other name under heaven that has been given among men, by which we must be saved" (Acts 4:12). Jesus's ministry, including His ministry of reconciliation in this current day, is a demonstration of the Father's grace and mercy as expressed in Exodus 34:5-9. "But the present heavens and earth by His word are being reserved for fire, kept for the Day of Judgment and destruction of ungodly men. But do not let this one fact escape your notice, beloved, that with the Lord one day is as a thousand years, and a thousand years as one day. The Lord is not slow about His promise, as some count slowness, but is patient toward you, not wishing for any to perish but for all to come to repentance" (2 Peter 3:7-9).

What Shall We Say Then?

The Bible is clear. The whole world is in need of a savior! And the only source for a savior is God Himself, Whom the world does not know. Because He loves us so, God sent His only begotten

Son, Jesus, into the world to pay the penalty for the entire world's disobedience. And after He paid it, God has turned to us in our sin soaked, sin sick state. He is offering each of us forgiveness of sins and the gift of eternal life through belief and confidence in, and surrender of our lives to, His Son. If you are willing, humble yourself and submit to Him and accept His free gift before it is everlastingly too late!

Eternal horror or eternal joy awaits you. Your lack of action is a choice for eternal horror. Therefore, I beg you, choose eternal joy. Choose to believe Jesus Christ. Amen. Amen. Amen!!!

Please take a few minutes right now to listen to the message, The Other Side of Death by clicking the message's title on biblethreads.net.

* * * * *

PRAYER: Heavenly Father, Your love for us is so amazing. "The Lord's lovingkindnesses indeed never cease, For His compassions never fail. They are new every morning; Great is Your faithfulness" (Lamentations 3:22-23). Your relentless pursuit of us is incredible. May Your name be forever glorified in the earth.

In the name of Love, Your Son Jesus, we ask that You would open the eyes of everyone who reads or is taught any portion of the books in this series, and give them a passion to study them, and then, give them an exceedingly great passion to study Your Word – the Bible. Give them the grace to study it from Your perspective, within a proper context, with understanding and with insight. Teach them, Father, that they may come to know You intimately. Let them see Your truth through Your eyes.

Finally, Father, we ask that You would please lead each of them into the life that is only in Your Son. In Jesus name we pray. And just as we have spoken, so let it be done. Thank you, Father, for the blessings already on the way. Amen!!

Part 3

Conclusion

But God demonstrates His own love toward us, in that while we were yet sinners, Christ died for us. Much more then, having now been justified by His blood, we shall be saved from the wrath of God through Him. For if while we were enemies, we were reconciled to God through the death of His Son, much more, having been reconciled, we shall be saved by His life.
Romans 5:8-10.

Your Special Invitation

If you do not have a personal relationship with our Savior and Lord, *JESUS*, or if you are not certain where you will spend eternity, please take some time right now to review the article by Dr. Thomas L. Constable, <u>Have You Heard the Good News From the Bible?</u>.

Receive Jesus Christ In Your Heart

Welcome back! Have you accepted Christ? If not, are you willing to humble yourself before God and submit yourself to Him? Let Him know you want to receive His Son, Jesus, the Christ, into your heart; and you want to accept His "free gift" of eternal life with Him. All it takes is a sincere heart and your confidence that *God truly is Who He says He is and that God will do exactly what He says He will do.* Open your mouth and speak to Him now as if you were standing before Him. Ask for His forgiveness. Acknowledge that you have rejected Him in the past. You chose to go your own way. Confess the sins you know about and acknowledge those you don't. Ask Him to teach you how to love Him. He is eagerly waiting to hear from you! So do it now! Right now! Please, do not wait another day! This is far too important! The quality of your life in eternity is at stake. Today could very well be your last day. Eternity could begin for you at any moment. So do it now! You must do it while you are still in your body.

If you have confessed your sins and accepted Jesus into your life as a result of studying this book and/or the referenced Internet articles, please let us know that you have by contacting us on our blog, www.arlingtonmcrae.org (Contact page), or texting the word "**NewBeliever**" (no space, no quotation marks) to **31996**. Later, if you reply to our confirmation with your email address (email is not required; personal information will remain private), we have a special gift we would love to send to you via email.

Thank you for receiving Jesus Christ into your life. It is the work of the Holy Spirit of Christ. To Him be the glory forever and ever! Amen!

Now learn of Him by conversing with Him and studying His Bible daily. Commit to living a life that honors Him in the church, at school, in the market place (the mall, business dealings, etc.), on your job, and in your family and social life, including social media sites. Find a Bible based church that is committed to Jesus' ministry of reconciliation and immerse yourself in it (2 Corinthians 5:17-21). That is the least you should do for the love and grace (divine favor and power) Jesus has shown you. In the meantime, see the free online book, <u>Christian Basic Training</u> by Charles T. Buntin. Additionally, I recommend you study the articles under the title, <u>Basics of Christian Faith</u> by Vickie Kraft.

Still Not Convinced?

If all this still makes no sense to you, please, don't stop now! Jump right into the set of articles under the title, <u>A Not-So-Brief Defense of Christianity</u> by Jimmy Williams. Also explore the related topic, "Apologetics", on the same page.

Now, having read the above referenced articles by Jimmy Williams and others, are you still not convinced? Then, I strongly recommend you pray to Jesus as if He is real and ask Him to draw you to Himself. You might say something like this: "Jesus, I just cannot see how You can be real and how the Bible can be true. All this Bible stuff makes no sense to me. It's all fairy tales. Plus, it's giving me a headache. So if You are real, please be real to me and come into my heart. Open my eyes that I might see clearly. Amen."

If you prayed with reverence, sincerity, humility, and expectancy, look for a miracle. It may not manifest today, but it will come if you continue to pray this prayer daily, with a sincere heart, expecting an answer. So look for a change! Study the full content of this book and the online references again. In addition, search the vast content at the <u>www.bible.org</u> website where you will find answers to many of your questions, though certainly not all. Some answers can only come from Jesus Christ Himself. So continue to talk to Him, no matter what, no matter how you feel or what you think. Let Him know you are not going to quit bothering Him until you are certain you have eternal life with Him. And finally, rebuke and renounce the influence of the devil in your life. Oh! You don't believe in Satan either? That's OK. Just act like he's real too!

If you simply cannot allow yourself to accept Jesus at this time, continue to study the Bible. You might begin by studying the books of John, Romans, and Ephesians. Then go to Genesis and read straight through to Revelation. Choose a Bible based church and attend services each Sunday and during the week. Get into their basic Bible study classes and ask thought provoking questions that are dear to your heart. Continue to study future books in this series as they come available and put into practice what you learn. At the same time, share this book and the Bible with other like-minded people. Discuss it and debate it with them. And may Jesus continue His work in you until you are ready to humble yourself and receive His kindness.

May you come to experience His abundant love for you despite the extent of your sins. **He truly loves you just as you are!** But He is not willing for you to remain as you are. He has a better life in store for you. I know it's hard to believe. Nevertheless, it is true!

Spiritual Forces Are at Work
Jesus Teaches in Parables

1 On that day Jesus went out of the house, and was sitting by the sea. 2And great multitudes gathered to

Him, so that He got into a boat and sat down, and the whole multitude was standing on the beach. 3And He spoke many things to them in parables, saying, "Behold, the **sower** went out to sow; 4and as he sowed, some seeds fell beside the road, and the birds came and ate them up. 5" And others fell upon the rocky places, where they did not have much soil; and immediately they sprang up, because they had no depth of soil. 6" But when the sun had risen, they were scorched; and because they had no root, they withered away. 7" And others fell among the thorns, and the thorns came up and choked them out. 8" And others fell on the good soil, and yielded a crop, some a hundredfold, some sixty, and some thirty. 9" He who has ears, let him hear."

18" Hear then the parable of the **sower**. 19" When anyone hears **the word** of the kingdom, and does not understand it, the evil one comes and snatches away what has been sown in his heart. This is the one on whom **seed** was sown beside the road. 20" And the one on whom seed was sown on the rocky places, this is the man who hears the word, and immediately receives it with joy; 21yet he has no firm root in himself, but is only temporary, and when affliction or persecution arises because of the word, immediately he falls away. 22" And the one on whom seed was sown among the thorns, this is the man who hears the word, and the worry of the world, and the deceitfulness of riches choke the word, and it becomes unfruitful. 23" And the one on whom seed was sown on the good soil, this is the man who hears the word and understands it; who indeed bears fruit, and brings forth, some a hundredfold, some sixty, and some thirty." (Matthew 13:1-9, 18-23) [Emphasis mine].

PRAYER: Heavenly Father, in the name of Your Son, Jesus, we honor You and we praise You for Your kindness toward evil men and women. You cause Your sun to shine on the evil as well as the righteous. Thank You for those who already have accepted Your Son as their Savior as a result of this book. And we beseech You now on behalf of all our brothers and sisters all over the earth who just can't seem to perceive and accept Your truth and Your Son. We ask You, in Your love and in Your grace (Your divine favor and power), to pierce the darkness, remove the chains, lift the blindness, and release their souls to receive your Son. We realize we don't deserve Your selfless love. So we don't ask on our account, but on account You abound in lovingkindness, compassion, and mercy. Your mercies are new every morning. We are confident You know how to give every good and perfect gift to Your children who ask of You. Therefore, we give You thanks for it now. And thank You Lord Jesus for Your sacrifice. May all mankind glorify Your name. May You be forever praised in the earth. Amen and amen!

Closing Words

As we close, I have some final questions especially for believers. I urge you to answer these questions aloud. I just want you to answer them honestly for yourself.

My Final Questions

If you will, place a Bible in your hand. Now, take a good look at the book you are holding in your hand (the Bible). Look at it from all sides. I want to make sure you appreciate what it is. Therefore, let me ask you this question: "Do you accept the Bible as the Word of the true and living God, Yahweh?" Let me reiterate. "Do you honestly and truly believe that the Bible is in fact the written revelation of the only true and living God?"

The second question I want to ask you is this: "Do you believe that the Bible is without error in the original manuscripts?" The original manuscripts are the writings of the original authors as they received revelation through the Holy Spirit. Examples of original manuscripts are those that Moses wrote as a result of hearing from God. That was the original manuscript. You may argue with me that there are errors in this Bible you are holding in your hand. Well, that is possible. In language translations, many decisions have to be made, is it this or is it that. But we do know that even the Holy Spirit participates in the translating process minimizing errors. So my question is, "Do you believe that the Bible is without error in its original manuscripts?" Think about it! Search deep within your heart! Reason with yourself!

The above questions go to the heart of the doctrine of bibliology. If need be, study the articles in the series, Bibliology – The Doctrine of the Written Word by J. Hampton Keathley III. Also, review the article, Bibliology: The Bible by Greg Herrick. Your acceptance of the authority of the Bible is essential for a full understanding.

Now, if you tell me, "Yes, I believe the Bible in my hand is the Word of God". And if you tell me, "Yes, I believe that it is better than 99% accurate". (Don't let a minute percentage of possible errors keep you out of God's heaven. So often, perceived errors are caused by a lack of knowledge on the reader's part or intentional deception by others.) Then the final question I have for you is this: **"What role does this Bible play in your life?"** You tell me you believe the Bible is the Word of God. You tell me you believe that it is without error. So now, the question is, do your actions say you believe what your tongue has declared? As you attempt to answer this question, don't just look at yourself. Look at somebody else who knows you well, and ask yourself,

"Would that person say my actions say that I truly believe the Bible is the Word of God; and I believe it is without error?" Please answer these questions honestly for yourself. Take some time to meditate on the implications of your answers. Let's get that settled right here, right now. Your answers here will greatly affect how well you will spend eternity. It may very well determine your acceptance of future lessons in this series.

Bible Study

To assist you in gaining a comprehensive understanding of the Bible, I am providing links to the following study resources for your convenience. With the exception of "BE101 Bible Study Methods & Hermeneutics" and "The Bible Knowledge Commentary", all of the following referenced study materials are offered without endorsement of the author(s)' presentation or theology. I pray they will be a tremendous aid to you in discovering God's truth for yourself while enjoying your journey. I would appreciate hearing how they have helped you or not at all.

For lessons in Bible study techniques and supporting study resources, consider the following courses, articles, and books:

BE101 Bible Study Methods & Hermeneutics, a video presentation by Dr. Mark Bailey, President of Dallas Theological Seminary. Click the "View In iTunes" link for a free download from iTunes. This is a thorough, college level, video presentation of the inductive Bible study method.

You Can Understand the Bible: An Introduction to and Application of the Contextual/Textual Method of Biblical

Interpretation (Hermeneutics) by Dr. Bob Utley, Professor of Hermeneutics.

The Bible Knowledge Commentary: An Exposition of the Scriptures by Dallas Seminary Faculty, 2 Volumes Old & New Testament by John Walvoord and Roy Zuck.

Wiersbe Bible Commentary, 2 Vol Set w/CD Rom, New Edition by Dr. Warren W. Wiersbe as well as other resources by Dr. Wiersbe.

Free Bible Commentary by Dr. Bob Utley, Professor of Hermeneutics. Click the www.FreeBibleCommentary.org link in the home page.

How to Read the Bible for All Its Worth: A Guide to Understanding the Bible by Gordon D. Fee & Douglas Stuart. I discovered this book by reading website reviews. The book is available at major book outlets.

Also see the article, Studying the Scriptures by Kenneth Boa. Use the bible.org website for extensive Bible resources on a broad range of subjects. On the Home Page, click the menu buttons – Study or Resources – in the middle of the page. You may also access other links at the bottom of the page. Or, use the search bar to reveal articles on a particular word, passage of Scripture, or subject.

Document Your Understanding

I encourage you once again to make copious notes during your studies and review them often. Talk about them. Analyze them. Meditate on them. Debate them with yourself, your spouse, your children, and your siblings, as well as with friends and associates. Use these debates to clarify and reinforce your understanding and recall of all the concepts presented in this book and in the Bible. If you stay in His Word, and in prayer, God will guide your study and He will give you an illuminated insight into His Word, if you ask Him. When He does, be certain to write down what He gives you exactly as He gives it to you. Usually, it is not meant just for you. So, remember to share it as would a priest for the Most High God. Help others to prosper in God's Word as you prosper. I exhort you to take this knowledge with you for the rest of your life. Keep it in the forefront of your mind. Recall it to mind especially when you sit down to study and meditate on the Scriptures; and when you discuss Scriptures with others. If you do, your reward will be great! I sincerely believe it will change your life both in the here and now and throughout eternity. May Jesus, the Christ, richly bless everything you set your mind to do for His kingdom? Amen!

Share Your Thoughts

It's now your time to give back. If this book has benefited you in the slightest way or not at all, we would love to hear from you. Please make it a priority to post your book review at www.amazon.com as well as other retailers' and book review websites such as Barnes & Noble, iTunes, and Goodreads. Please tweet and post often about your newfound biblical understanding on all your social networking sites. Encourage them to study and apply this series.

Additionally, we would love to interact with you on our blogs at www.biblethreads.net or www.arlingtonmcrae.org. Thank you in advance for sacrificing your time to help us help others understand the message of the life-giving Bible!

Worldwide Ambassadors

I am one who believes that God does not give one person all the knowledge and all the talent, or all of anything. The apostle Paul, speaking of Christians, says that we are all like parts of a body. My foot is not all that my body needs. The foot is not capable of doing everything my body needs. Nor was it made for that purpose. I have a purpose and you have a purpose. Therefore, I invite you to make your own mark on the world. Come join with us to create a worldwide spiritual movement of Bible believing ambassadors for Jesus Christ; whose goal is to see the Bible through God's eyes and God's heart, then live accordingly, and to invite others to do the same. Begin right now, today, if you haven't already done so, by recruiting yourself a study partner or several partners. As you are doing your group study of this book, you and your partner(s) can begin applying what you have learned, to study the Bible more intelligently. Then make it your business to share your knowledge enthusiastically with everyone you know and with strangers who will listen. With today's Internet technology, we can make friends all around the globe through social media and micro blogging sites, etc. I encourage you to use this technology to bless people wherever they are, to the glory of our holy God and His beloved Son, Jesus Christ!

Your Final questions?

Remember to write them down now. Please, don't put it off. Reward yourself by documenting your questions and answers and Jesus will reward you too, if you ask Him (Matthew 7:7-8).

What's Next?

In our next volume, we are going to explore in detail some of the things we talked about here. We shall concentrate much (but certainly not all) of that study in the first six chapters of the Bible. So, in anticipation of the next set of lessons, I am asking you to please read the first six chapters of the Bible, slowly and very carefully, perhaps seven or eight times, or more. Meditate on each verse, phrase and thought. Moreover, if you are energetic, go on and read the first twelve chapters seven or eight times.

Now, you might ask, "Why are we spending all this time and effort in the very first part of Genesis?" Well, let me ask you a question, "How many times have you heard a pastor preach on the first five chapters in the Bible?" "You don't hear it very often, do you?" I have attended services at a number of churches. And I would dare say I have heard not more than three sermons devoted primarily to the first five chapters of Genesis. So let me give you a little enthusiasm for Genesis. God told me to read and study, and make sure I know the books of John. So, for more than a year, I studied the books of John and 1 John. Until finally, I got to the point where I said, "God, I think I have gotten all I can get on my own. I know I don't have everything. But whatever else there is, You are going to have to show me." So then, God said to me, "Study Genesis". Now, I had noticed that John seems to be directing the reader back to Genesis. Why do I say that? In the first verse of John, 1:1, we read, "In the beginning…" Those three words right there, to me, are directing the reader back to Genesis in that John begins his book with the exact same words found in Genesis 1:1, with reference to creation. John wanted his readers to keep the creation narrative, and its immediate aftermath, in focus as they read. As I said, I had gotten what I could from John.

"Study Genesis"

This is going to sound silly, I know. But, I spent nearly three years studying the first six chapters of the Bible, i.e., Genesis chapters 1 through 6. I was in seminary and working full time. Therefore, I was studying many other books. But every time I had some free time when I was able to read what I wanted to read, I was reading and researching, and meditating primarily on the first six chapters in the book of Genesis. Now you might say, "What the heck could you get out of those first six chapters to study them for three years?" Well, maybe I am simply a slow learner. Or maybe my head is a hard nut to crack. But I would answer you this way. The first eleven chapters in the book of Genesis set the stage for the rest of the entire Bible. I remember when I first heard my seminary professor say that. I thought, "I don't see how that can be." So I obeyed God and I studied, studied, and studied, carefully observing each word, phrase and thought. What is my conclusion? The first eleven chapters, in the book of Genesis, set the stage for everything that occurs in the Bible from that point forward. That simple fact tells me that we as Christians and students of God's Word, or God seekers, if we would understand the program of

God and our role in it, we have to understand the foundation that sets the stage for the program of God.

* * * * *

FINAL PRAYER: Heavenly Father, in the name of Jesus, we thank You for the opportunities to study Your Word, to learn Your Word as it is intended to be known. We realize, Father, at this stage, that it is just a lot of information for many of Your readers. We realize that our hearts and minds may not yet agree with the insights You have given us. And we realize that the deceiver is saying to someone even now, "Ah, this is too much stuff! You don't need to know all this; it doesn't mean that much anyway"! But we know You are able to help us see the truth in spite of the deceiver. We know, Father, You are able to help us overcome anything that the deceiver puts in our way. So we are asking You not because of anything in us, but because of Your heart, because of Who You are. We are asking You to help us; to give us a heart that desires to know You. Put in us, Father, a yearning for the knowledge of You. We are asking You to give us knowledge. Give us understanding and insight so that we would treasure it, live it, and teach it. And we ask You, heavenly Father, to give us wisdom. Your Word tells us that if any man (or woman) lacks wisdom, let him ask (James 1:5). And you will give to us in abundance. So right now, this day, we are asking for Your wisdom that we may in turn glorify You.

In addition, we are asking You to give us a burning and passionate desire to know Your Word. For we know that if we know Your Word, we will come to know You like You truly are, the compassionate God Who knows us better than we know ourselves; the God Who loves us in spite of who we are. We know, Father, that our knowing You will give us peace and bring joy to Your heart.

And, Father, we desire to share what You have given us with a great many multitudes, in every country, all over the world. Therefore, we ask that You would give us favor and cause these words to be distributed, read, debated, and accepted over the whole earth so that all the peoples of the earth may gain knowledge, understanding, and wisdom; and come to know Your Son, Jesus, in the salvation of their souls. For each person who reads or hears any portion of the books in this series, we ask You to change their lives through the knowledge of Your Word; and that they would, in turn, help change the lives of others through proclamation of Your Word and their witness. For we know that You did not save us just for ourselves. You did not save us so You could heap Your blessings solely upon those You saved. But You have saved us to be a life-giving spirit to the rest of the world. We pray that You will make it so in our lives. Sanctify us to Your purpose. Cause us to subordinate our desires to Your desires. Overshadow our will. Give us a willing heart and a willing spirit. Give us a passion to do Your will. And give us grace to accomplish Your work.

Merciful Father, this week and in the months to come, we know there will be obstacles to keep us from studying the first six or the first twelve chapters of the Bible, even your entire revelation. We know the evil one has already put obstacles in our

172

way. He is going to create distractions, create burdensome situations, and create conflict. But Father, we know You are able to quell all the contention, controversy, and frustration, and to remove all obstacles. You are able to give us the peace that surpasses all understanding. And You are able to set aside time in our lives so that we may diligently study Your Word; so that we may learn of You. So give us great enthusiasm for what we have gained thus far from studying this book; and give us recall and great zeal to apply what we have learned to the daily study of Your Bible.

Finally, Father, present to us a reading plan to guide us in reading through the entire Bible, at least once, within the next twelve months. Do not allow us to become discouraged when we don't fully understand what we are reading. But empower us to press on any way until we learn that the Bible explains the Bible. And we must read it in its entirety if we are to experience that truth.

We thank You. We give You the praise. We give You the glory. And we will magnify Your name for all that You have done, for all that You are doing, and for all that You will do in the months, years, and decades to come. May Your name be forever glorified in the earth! In the mighty, the awesome name of Your Son, Jesus, the Christ, we pray. Amen!

For this reason I too, having heard of the faith in the Lord Jesus which exists among you, and your love for all the saints, 16 do not cease giving thanks for you, while making mention of you in my prayers; 17 that the God of our Lord Jesus Christ, the Father of glory, may give to you a spirit of wisdom and of revelation in the knowledge of Him. 18 I pray that the eyes of your heart may be enlightened, so that you will know what is the hope of His calling, what are the riches of the glory of His inheritance in the saints, 19 and what is the surpassing greatness of His power toward us who believe. These are in accordance with the working of the strength of His might 20 which He brought about in Christ, when He raised Him from the dead and seated Him at His right hand in the heavenly places, 21 far above all rule and authority and power and dominion, and every name that is named, not only in this age but also in the one to come. 22 And He put all things in subjection under His feet, and gave Him as head over all things to the church, 23 which is His body, the fullness of Him who fills all in all (Ephesians 1:15-23).

Appendix: Referenced Scriptures

(1 Peter 4:1-3) Therefore, since Christ has suffered in the flesh, arm yourselves also with the same purpose, because he who has suffered in the flesh has ceased from sin, 2so as to live the rest of the time in the flesh no longer for the lusts of men, but for the will of God. 3For the time already past is sufficient for you to have carried out the desire of the Gentiles, having pursued a course of sensuality, lusts, drunkenness, carousing, drinking parties and abominable idolatries. (1 Peter 4:1-3).

(1 Samuel 3:1-9) Now the boy Samuel was ministering to the LORD before Eli. And word from the LORD was rare in those days, visions were infrequent. 2And it happened at that time as Eli was lying down in his place (now his eyesight had begun to grow dim and he could not see well), 3and the lamp of God had not yet gone out, and Samuel was lying down in the temple of the LORD where the ark of God was, 4that the LORD called Samuel; and he said, "Here I am." 5Then he ran to Eli and said, "Here I am, for you called me." But he said, "I did not call, lie down again." So he went and lay down. 6And the LORD called yet again, "Samuel!" So Samuel arose and went to Eli, and said, "Here I am, for you called me." But he answered, "I did not call, my son, lie down

again." 7Now Samuel did not yet know the LORD, nor had the word of the LORD yet been revealed to him. 8So the LORD called Samuel again for the third time. And he arose and went to Eli, and said, "Here I am, for you called me." Then Eli discerned that the LORD was calling the boy. 9And Eli said to Samuel, "Go lie down, and it shall be if He calls you, that you shall say, 'Speak, LORD, for Your servant is listening.' " So Samuel went and lay down in his place. (1 Samuel 3:1-9).

(1 Thessalonians 5:16-18) Rejoice always; 17pray without ceasing; 18in everything give thanks; for this is God's will for you in Christ Jesus. (1 Thessalonians 5:16-18).

(1 Peter 2:9-12) But you are A CHOSEN RACE, A royal PRIESTHOOD, A HOLY NATION, A PEOPLE FOR God's OWN POSSESSION, that you may proclaim the excellencies of Him who has called you out of darkness into His marvelous light; 10for you once were NOT A PEOPLE, but now you are THE PEOPLE OF GOD; you had NOT RECEIVED MERCY, but now you have RECEIVED MERCY. 11 Beloved, I urge you as aliens and strangers to abstain from fleshly lusts, which wage war against the soul. 12Keep your behavior excellent among the Gentiles, so that in the thing in which they slander you as evildoers, they may on account of your good deeds, as they observe them, glorify God in the day of visitation. (1 Peter 2:9-12).

(Matthew 4:1-4) Then Jesus was led up by the Spirit into the wilderness to be tempted by the devil. 2And after He had fasted forty days and forty nights, He then became hungry. 3And the tempter came and said to Him, "If You are the Son of God, command that these stones become bread." 4But He answered and said, "It is written, 'MAN SHALL NOT LIVE ON BREAD ALONE, BUT ON EVERY WORD THAT PROCEEDS OUT OF THE MOUTH OF GOD.' " (Matthew 4:1-4).

(Matthew 7:7-8) "Ask, and it shall be given to you; seek, and you shall find; knock, and it shall be opened to you. 8" For everyone who asks receives, and he who seeks finds, and to him who knocks it shall be opened." (Matthew 7:7-8).

(2 Corinthians 5:14-21) For the love of Christ controls us, having concluded this, that one died for all, therefore all died; 15and He died for all, that they who live should no longer live for themselves, but for Him who died and rose again on their behalf. 16Therefore from now on we recognize no man according to the flesh; even though we have known Christ according to the flesh, yet now we know Him thus no longer. 17Therefore if any man is in Christ, he is a new creature; the old things passed away; behold, new things have come. 18Now all these things are from God, who reconciled us to Himself through Christ, and gave us the ministry of reconciliation, 19namely, that God was in Christ reconciling the world to Himself, not counting their trespasses against them, and He has committed to us the word of reconciliation. 20 Therefore, we are ambassadors for Christ, as though God were entreating through us; we beg you on behalf of Christ, be reconciled to God. 21He made Him who knew no sin to be sin on our behalf, that we might become the righteousness of God in Him. (2 Corinthians 5:14-21).

(Matthew 28:16-20) The Great Commission. But the eleven disciples proceeded to Galilee, to the mountain which Jesus had designated. 17And when they saw Him, they worshiped Him; but some were doubtful. 18And Jesus came up and spoke to them, saying, "All authority has been given to Me in heaven and on earth. 19" Go therefore and make disciples of all the nations, baptizing them in the name of the Father and the Son and the Holy Spirit, 20teaching them to observe all that I commanded you; and lo, I am with you always, even to the end of the age." (Matthew 28:16-20).

(Jeremiah 11:1-11) The Broken Covenant: The word which came to Jeremiah from the LORD, saying, 2" Hear the words of this covenant, and speak to the men of Judah and to the inhabitants of Jerusalem; 3and say to them, 'Thus says the LORD, the God of Israel, "Cursed is the man who does not heed the words of this covenant 4which I commanded your forefathers in the day that I brought them out of the land of Egypt, from the iron furnace, saying, 'Listen to My voice, and do according to all which I command you; so you shall be My people, and I will be your God,' 5 in order to confirm the oath which I swore to your forefathers, to give them a land flowing with milk and honey, as it is this day." ' " Then I answered and said, "Amen, O LORD." 6 And the LORD said to me, "Proclaim all these words in the cities of Judah and in the streets of Jerusalem, saying, 'Hear the words of this covenant and do them. 7' For I solemnly warned your fathers in the day that I brought them up from the land of Egypt, even to this day, warning persistently, saying, "Listen to My voice." 8' Yet they did not obey or incline their ear, but walked, each one, in the stubbornness of his evil heart; therefore I brought on them all the words of this covenant, which I commanded them to do, but they did not.' 9 Then the LORD said to me, "A conspiracy has been found among the men of Judah and among the inhabitants of Jerusalem. 10" They have turned back to the iniquities of their ancestors who refused to hear My words, and they have gone after other gods to serve them; the house of Israel and the house of Judah have broken My covenant which I made with their fathers." 11Therefore thus says the LORD, "Behold I am bringing disaster on them which they will not be able to escape". (Jeremiah 11:1-11).

(1 Kings 11:1-13) Now King Solomon loved many foreign women along with the daughter of Pharaoh: Moabite, Ammonite, Edomite, Sidonian, and Hittite women, 2from the nations concerning which the LORD had said to the sons of Israel, "You shall not associate with them, neither shall they associate with you, for they will surely turn your heart away after their gods." Solomon held fast to these in love. 3And he had seven hundred wives, princesses, and three hundred concubines, and his wives turned his heart away. 4For it came about when Solomon was old, his wives turned his heart away after other gods; and his heart was not wholly devoted to the LORD his God, as the heart of David his father had been. 5For Solomon went after Ashtoreth the goddess of the Sidonians and after Milcom the detestable idol of the Ammonites. 6And Solomon did what was evil in the sight of the LORD, and did not follow the LORD fully, as David his father had done. 7Then Solomon built a high place for Chemosh the detestable idol of Moab, on the mountain which is east of Jerusalem, and for Molech the detestable idol of the sons of Ammon. 8Thus also he did for all his foreign wives, who burned incense and sacrificed to their gods. 9Now the LORD was angry with Solomon because his heart was turned away from the LORD,

the God of Israel, who had appeared to him twice, 10and had commanded him concerning this thing, that he should not go after other gods; but he did not observe what the LORD had commanded. 11So the LORD said to Solomon, "Because you have done this, and you have not kept My covenant and My statutes, which I have commanded you, I will surely tear the kingdom from you, and will give it to your servant. 12" Nevertheless I will not do it in your days for the sake of your father David, but I will tear it out of the hand of your son. 13" However, I will not tear away all the kingdom, but I will give one tribe to your son for the sake of My servant David and for the sake of Jerusalem which I have chosen." (1 Kings 11:1-13).

(Daniel 7:13-14) "I kept looking in the night visions, And behold, with the clouds of heaven One like a Son of Man was coming, And He came up to the Ancient of Days And was presented before Him. 14" And to Him was given dominion, Glory and a kingdom, That all the peoples, nations, and men of every language Might serve Him. His dominion is an everlasting dominion Which will not pass away; And His kingdom is one Which will not be destroyed. (Daniel 7:13-14).

(Luke 21:25-27) "And there will be signs in sun and moon and stars, and upon the earth dismay among nations, in perplexity at the roaring of the sea and the waves, 26men fainting from fear and the expectation of the things which are coming upon the world; for the powers of the heavens will be shaken. 27"And then they will see THE SON OF MAN COMING IN A CLOUD with power and great glory. 28" But when these things begin to take place, straighten up and lift up your heads, because your redemption is drawing near." (Luke 21:25-27).

(John 1:1-18) In the beginning was the Word, and the Word was with God, and the Word was God. 2He was in the beginning with God. 3All things came into being by Him, and apart from Him nothing came into being that has come into being. 4In Him was life, and the life was the light of men. 5And the light shines in the darkness, and the darkness did not comprehend it. 6 There came a man, sent from God, whose name was John. 7He came for a witness, that he might bear witness of the light, that all might believe through him. 8He was not the light, but came that he might bear witness of the light. 9 There was the true light which, coming into the world, enlightens every man. 10He was in the world, and the world was made through Him, and the world did not know Him. 11He came to His own, and those who were His own did not receive Him. 12But as many as received Him, to them He gave the right to become children of God, even to those who believe in His name, 13who were born not of blood, nor of the will of the flesh, nor of the will of man, but of God. 13The Word Made Flesh 14 And the Word became flesh, and dwelt among us, and we beheld His glory, glory as of the only begotten from the Father, full of grace and truth. 15John bore witness of Him, and cried out, saying, "This was He of whom I said, 'He who comes after me has a higher rank than I, for He existed before me.'" 16For of His fullness we have all received, and grace upon grace. 17For the Law was given through Moses; grace and truth were realized through Jesus Christ. 18No man has seen God at any time; the only begotten God, who is in the bosom of the Father, He has explained Him. (John 1:1-18).

(Isaiah 9:2) The people who walk in darkness Will see a great light; Those who live in a dark land, The light will shine on them. (Isaiah 9:2).

(John 8:12) Again therefore Jesus spoke to them, saying, "I am the light of the world; he who follows Me shall not walk in the darkness, but shall have the light of life." (John 8:12).

(Deuteronomy 18:15-19) "The LORD your God will raise up for you a prophet like me from among you, from your countrymen, you shall listen to him. 16" This is according to all that you asked of the LORD your God in Horeb on the day of the assembly, saying, 'Let me not hear again the voice of the LORD my God, let me not see this great fire anymore, lest I die.' 17" And the LORD said to me, 'They have spoken well. 18' I will raise up a prophet from among their countrymen like you, and I will put My words in his mouth, and he shall speak to them all that I command him. 19' And it shall come about that whoever will not listen to My words which he shall speak in My name, I Myself will require it of him. (Deuteronomy 18:15-19).

(John 8:26, 28) "I have many things to speak and to judge concerning you, but He who sent Me is true; and the things which I heard from Him, these I speak to the world." 27They did not realize that He had been speaking to them about the Father. 28Jesus therefore said, "When you lift up the Son of Man, then you will know that I am He, and I do nothing on My own initiative, but I speak these things as the Father taught Me. (John 8:26, 28).

(John 12:44-50) And Jesus cried out and said, "He who believes in Me does not believe in Me, but in Him who sent Me.

45" And he who beholds Me beholds the One who sent Me. 46" I have come as light into the world, that everyone who believes in Me may not remain in darkness. 47" And if anyone hears My sayings, and does not keep them, I do not judge him; for I did not come to judge the world, but to save the world. 48" He who rejects Me, and does not receive My sayings, has one who judges him; the word I spoke is what will judge him at the last day. 49" For I did not speak on My own initiative, but the Father Himself who sent Me has given Me commandment, what to say, and what to speak. 50" And I know that His commandment is eternal life; therefore the things I speak, I speak just as the Father has told Me." (John 12:44-50).

(Colossians 1:15-16) And He is the image of the invisible God, the first-born of all creation. 16For by Him all things were created, both in the heavens and on earth, visible and invisible, whether thrones or dominions or rulers or authorities— all things have been created by Him and for Him. (Colossians 1:15-16).

(Hebrews 1:1-4). 1 God, after He spoke long ago to the fathers in the prophets in many portions and in many ways, 2in these last days has spoken to us in His Son, whom He appointed heir of all things, through whom also He made the world. 3And He is the radiance of His glory and the exact representation of His nature, and upholds all things by the word of His power. When He had made purification of sins, He sat down at the right hand of the Majesty on high; 4having become as much better than the angels, as He has inherited a more excellent name than they. (Hebrews 1:1-4).

(John 17:6-8) "I manifested Your name to the men whom You

gave Me out of the world; Yours they were, and You gave them to Me, and they have kept Your word. 7" Now they have come to know that everything You have given Me is from You; 8for the words which You gave Me I have given to them; and they received them, and truly understood that I came forth from You, and they believed that You did send Me. (John 17:6-8).

(Mark 6:33-44) And the people saw them going, and many recognized them, and they ran there together on foot from all the cities, and got there ahead of them. 34And when He went ashore, He saw a great multitude, and He felt compassion for them because they were like sheep without a shepherd; and He began to teach them many things. 35And when it was already quite late, His disciples came up to Him and began saying, "The place is desolate and it is already quite late; 36send them away so that they may go into the surrounding countryside and villages and buy themselves something to eat." 37But He answered and said to them, "You give them something to eat!" And they said to Him, "Shall we go and spend two hundred denarii on bread and give them something to eat?" 38And He said to them, "How many loaves do you have? Go look!" And when they found out, they said, "Five and two fish." 39And He commanded them all to recline by groups on the green grass. 40And they reclined in companies of hundreds and of fifties. 41And He took the five loaves and the two fish, and looking up toward heaven, He blessed the food and broke the loaves and He kept giving them to the disciples to set before them; and He divided up the two fish among them all. 42And they all ate and were satisfied. 43And they picked up twelve full baskets of the broken pieces, and also of the fish. 44And there were five thousand men who ate the loaves. (Mark 6:33-44).

(Mark 8:1-9) In those days again, when there was a great multitude and they had nothing to eat, He called His disciples and said to them, 2" I feel compassion for the multitude because they have remained with Me now three days, and have nothing to eat; 3and if I send them away hungry to their home, they will faint on the way; and some of them have come from a distance." 4And His disciples answered Him, "Where will anyone be able to find enough to satisfy these men with bread here in a desolate place?" 5And He was asking them, "How many loaves do you have?" And they said, "Seven." 6And He *directed the multitude to sit down on the ground; and taking the seven loaves, He gave thanks and broke them, and started giving them to His disciples to serve to them, and they served them to the multitude. 7They also had a few small fish; and after He had blessed them, He ordered these to be served as well. 8And they ate and were satisfied; and they picked up seven large baskets full of what was left over of the broken pieces. 9And about four thousand were there; and He sent them away. (Mark 8:1-9).

(John 8:1-11) But Jesus went to the Mount of Olives. 2And early in the morning He came again into the temple, and all the people were coming to Him; and He sat down and began to teach them. 3And the scribes and the Pharisees brought a woman caught in adultery, and having set her in the midst, 4they said to Him, "Teacher, this woman has been caught in adultery, in the very act. 5" Now in the Law Moses commanded us to stone such women; what then do You say?" 6And they were saying this, testing Him, in order that they might have grounds for accusing Him. But Jesus stooped down, and with His finger wrote on the ground. 7But when they persisted in asking Him, He straightened up, and said to them, "He who is without sin among you, let him be the first to throw a stone at her." 8And again He stooped down, and wrote on the ground. 9And when they heard it, they began to go out one by one, beginning with the older ones, and He was left alone, and the woman, where she was, in the midst. 10And straightening up, Jesus said to her, "Woman, where are they? Did no one condemn you?" 11And she said, "No one, Lord." And Jesus said, "Neither do I condemn you; go your way. From now on sin no more.". (John 8:1-11).

(Acts 22:6-16) "And it came about that as I was on my way, approaching Damascus about noontime, a very bright light suddenly flashed from heaven all around me, 7and I fell to the ground and heard a voice saying to me, 'Saul, Saul, why are you persecuting Me?' 8" And I answered, 'Who are You, Lord?' And He said to me, 'I am Jesus the Nazarene, whom you are persecuting.' 9" And those who were with me beheld the light, to be sure, but did not understand the voice of the One who was speaking to me. 10" And I said, 'What shall I do, Lord?' And the Lord said to me, 'Arise and go on into Damascus; and there you will be told of all that has been appointed for you to do.' 11" But since I could not see because of the brightness of that light, I was led by the hand by those who were with me, and came into Damascus. 12" And a certain Ananias, a man who was devout by the standard of the Law, and well spoken of by all the Jews who lived there, 13came to me, and standing near said to me, 'Brother Saul, receive your sight!' And at that very time I looked up at him. 14" And he said, 'The God of our fathers has appointed you to know His will, and to see the Righteous One, and to hear an utterance from His mouth. 15' For you will be a witness for Him to all men of what you have seen and heard. 16' And now why do you delay? Arise, and be baptized, and wash away your sins, calling on His name.' (Acts 22:6-16).

(John 3:16-21) "For God so loved the world, that He gave His only begotten Son, that whoever believes in Him should not perish, but have eternal life. 17" For God did not send the Son into the world to judge the world, but that the world should be saved through Him. 18" He who believes in Him is not judged; he who does not believe has been judged already, because he has not believed in the name of the only begotten Son of God. 19" And this is the judgment, that the light is come into the world, and men loved the darkness rather than the light; for their deeds were evil. 20" For everyone who does evil hates the light, and does not come to the light, lest his deeds should be exposed. 21" But he who practices the truth comes to the light, that his deeds may be manifested as having been wrought in God." (John 3:16-21).

(Romans 5:1-17) Therefore having been justified by faith, we have peace with God through our Lord Jesus Christ, 2through whom also we have obtained our introduction by faith into this grace in which we stand; and we exult in hope of the glory of God. 3And not only this, but we also exult in our tribulations, knowing that tribulation brings about perseverance; 4and perseverance, proven character; and proven character, hope; 5and hope does not disappoint, because the love of God has been poured out within our hearts through the Holy Spirit who was given to us. 6For while we were still helpless, at the right time Christ died for the ungodly. 7For one will hardly die for a righteous man; though perhaps for the good man someone would dare even to die. 8But God demonstrates His own love toward us, in that while we were yet sinners, Christ died for us. 9Much more then, having now been justified by His blood, we shall be saved from the wrath of God through Him. 10For if while we were enemies, we were reconciled to God through the death of His Son, much more, having been reconciled, we shall be saved by His life. 11And not only this, but we also exult in God through our Lord Jesus Christ, through whom we have now received the reconciliation. 12 Therefore, just as through one man sin entered into the world, and death through sin, and so death spread to all men, because all sinned- 13for until the Law sin was in the world; but sin is not imputed when there is no law. 14Nevertheless death reigned from Adam until Moses, even over those who had not sinned in the likeness of the offense of Adam, who is a type of Him who was to come. 15But the free gift is not like the transgression. For if by the transgression of the one the many died, much more did the grace of God and the gift by the grace of the one Man, Jesus Christ, abound to the many. 16And the gift is not like that which came through the one who sinned; for on the one hand the judgment arose from one transgression resulting in condemnation, but on the other hand the free gift arose from many transgressions resulting in justification. 17For if by the transgression of the one, death reigned through the one, much more those who receive the abundance of grace and of the gift of righteousness will reign in life through the One, Jesus Christ. (Romans 5:1-17).

(Romans 6:20-23) For when you were slaves of sin, you were free in regard to righteousness. 21Therefore what benefit were you then deriving from the things of which you are now ashamed?

For the outcome of those things is death. 22But now having been freed from sin and enslaved to God, you derive your benefit, resulting in sanctification, and the outcome, eternal life. 23For the wages of sin is death, but the free gift of God is eternal life in Christ Jesus our Lord. (Romans 6:20-23).

(Ephesians 3:1-13) For this reason I, Paul, the prisoner of Christ Jesus for the sake of you Gentiles- 2if indeed you have heard of the stewardship of God's grace which was given to me for you; 3that by revelation there was made known to me the mystery, as I wrote before in brief. 4And by referring to this, when you read you can understand my insight into the mystery of Christ, 5which in other generations was not made known to the sons of men, as it has now been revealed to His holy apostles and prophets in the Spirit; 6to be specific, that the Gentiles are fellow heirs and fellow members of the body, and fellow partakers of the promise in Christ Jesus through the gospel, 7of which I was made a minister, according to the gift of God's grace which was given to me according to the working of His power. 8To me, the very least of all saints, this grace was given, to preach to the Gentiles the unfathomable riches of Christ, 9and to bring to light what is the administration of the mystery which for ages has been hidden in God, who created all things; 10in order that the manifold wisdom of God might now be made known through the church to the rulers and the authorities in the heavenly places. 11This was in accordance with the eternal purpose which He carried out in Christ Jesus our Lord, 12in whom we have boldness and confident access through faith in Him. 13Therefore I ask you not to lose heart at my tribulations on your behalf, for they are your glory. (Ephesians 3:1-13).

(1 John 4:7-11) Beloved, let us love one another, for love is from God; and everyone who loves is born of God and knows God. 8The one who does not love does not know God, for God is love. 9By this the love of God was manifested in us, that God has sent His only begotten Son into the world so that we might live through Him. 10In this is love, not that we loved God, but that He loved us and sent His Son to be the propitiation for our sins. 11Beloved, if God so loved us, we also ought to love one another. (1 John 4:7-11).

(John 8:39-40) They answered and said to Him, "Abraham is our father." Jesus *said to them, "If you are Abraham's children, do the deeds of Abraham. 40" But as it is, you are seeking to kill Me, a man who has told you the truth, which I heard from God; this Abraham did not do. (John 8:39-40).

(John 8:43-46) "Why do you not understand what I am saying? It is because you cannot hear My word. 44" You are of your father the devil, and you want to do the desires of your father. He was a murderer from the beginning, and does not stand in the truth, because there is no truth in him. Whenever he speaks a lie, he speaks from his own nature; for he is a liar, and the father of lies. 45" But because I speak the truth, you do not believe Me. 46" Which one of you convicts Me of sin? If I speak truth, why do you not believe Me? (John 8:43-46).

(John 14:16-17) "And I will ask the Father, and He will give you another Helper, that He may be with you forever; 17that is the Spirit of truth, whom the world cannot receive, because it does not behold Him or know Him, but you know Him because He abides with you, and will be in you. (John 14:16-17).

(Hebrews 3:1-3) Therefore, holy brethren, partakers of a heavenly calling, consider Jesus, the Apostle and High Priest of our confession. 2He was faithful to Him who appointed Him, as Moses also was in all His house. 3For He has been counted worthy of more glory than Moses, by just so much as the builder of the house has more honor than the house. (Hebrews 3:1-3).

(Deuteronomy 3:21-22) "And I commanded Joshua at that time, saying, 'Your eyes have seen all that the LORD your God has done to these two kings; so the LORD shall do to all the kingdoms into which you are about to cross. 22' Do not fear them, for the LORD your God is the one fighting for you.' (Deuteronomy 3:21-22).

(Deuteronomy 31:8) "And the LORD is the one who goes ahead of you; He will be with you. He will not fail you or forsake you. Do not fear, or be dismayed." (Deuteronomy 31:8).

(1 Timothy 2:14) And it was not Adam who was deceived, but the woman being quite deceived, fell into transgression. (1 Timothy 2:14).

(Isaiah 46:9-11) "Remember the former things long past, For I am God, and there is no other; I am God, and there is no one like Me, 10Declaring the end from the beginning And from ancient times things which have not been done, Saying, 'My purpose will be established, And I will accomplish all My good pleasure'; 11Calling a bird of prey from the east, The man of My purpose from a far country. Truly I have spoken; truly I will bring it to pass. I have planned it, surely I will do it. (Isaiah 46:9-11).

(Psalm 1) The Righteous and the Wicked Contrasted: How

blessed is the man who does not walk in the counsel of the wicked, Nor stand in the path of sinners, Nor sit in the seat of scoffers! 2But his delight is in the law of the LORD, And in His law he meditates day and night. 3And he will be like a tree firmly planted by streams of water, Which yields its fruit in its season, And its leaf does not wither; And in whatever he does, he prospers. 4 The wicked are not so, But they are like chaff which the wind drives away. 5Therefore the wicked will not stand in the judgment, Nor sinners in the assembly of the righteous. 6For the LORD knows the way of the righteous, But the way of the wicked will perish. (Psalm 1).

(Galatians 5:22-23) But the fruit of the Spirit is love, joy, peace, patience, kindness, goodness, faithfulness, 23gentleness, self-control; against such things there is no law. 24Now those who belong to Christ Jesus have crucified the flesh with its passions and desires. (Galatians 5:22-23).

(Exodus 34:6-7) Then the LORD passed by in front of him and proclaimed, "The LORD, the LORD God, compassionate and gracious, slow to anger, and abounding in lovingkindness and truth; 7who keeps lovingkindness for thousands, who forgives iniquity, transgression and sin; yet He will by no means leave the guilty unpunished, visiting the iniquity of fathers on the children and on the grandchildren to the third and fourth generations." (Exodus 34:6-7).

(Genesis 6:5-6) Then the LORD saw that the wickedness of man was great on the earth, and that every intent of the thoughts of his heart was only evil continually. 6And the LORD was sorry that He had made man on the earth, and He was grieved in His heart. (Genesis 6:5-6).

(Galatians 5:19-21) Now the deeds of the flesh are evident, which are: immorality, impurity, sensuality, 20idolatry, sorcery, enmities, strife, jealousy, outbursts of anger, disputes, dissensions, factions, 21envying, drunkenness, carousing, and things like these, of which I forewarn you just as I have forewarned you that those who practice such things shall not inherit the kingdom of God. (Galatians 5:19-21).

(2 Timothy 3:1-5) But realize this, that in the last days difficult times will come. 2For men will be lovers of self, lovers of money, boastful, arrogant, revilers, disobedient to parents, ungrateful, unholy, 3unloving, irreconcilable, malicious gossips, without self-control, brutal, haters of good, 4treacherous, reckless, conceited, lovers of pleasure rather than lovers of God; 5holding to a form of godliness, although they have denied its power; and avoid such men as these. (2 Timothy 3:1-5).

(Genesis 2:25) And the man and his wife were both naked and were not ashamed. (Genesis 2:25).

(Genesis 3:4-11) And the serpent said to the woman, "You surely shall not die! 5" For God knows that in the day you eat from it your eyes will be opened, and you will be like God, knowing good and evil." 6When the woman saw that the tree was good for food, and that it was a delight to the eyes, and that the tree was desirable to make one wise, she took from its fruit and ate; and she gave also to her husband with her, and he ate. 7Then the eyes of both of them were opened, and they knew that they were naked; and they sewed fig leaves together and made themselves loin coverings. 8 And they heard the sound of the

LORD God walking in the garden in the cool of the day, and the man and his wife hid themselves from the presence of the LORD God among the trees of the garden. 9Then the LORD God called to the man, and said to him, "Where are you?" 10And he said, "I heard the sound of You in the garden, and I was afraid because I was naked; so I hid myself." 11And He said, "Who told you that you were naked? Have you eaten from the tree of which I commanded you not to eat?" (Genesis 3:4-11).

(1 John 2:1-3, 23, 25) My little children, I am writing these things to you that you may not sin. And if anyone sins, we have an Advocate with the Father, Jesus Christ the righteous; 2and He Himself is the propitiation for our sins; and not for ours only, but also for those of the whole world. 3And by this we know that we have come to know Him, if we keep His commandments.

23Whoever denies the Son does not have the Father; the one who confesses the Son has the Father also.

25And this is the promise which He Himself made to us: eternal life. (1 John 2:1-3, 23, 25).

(1 John 3:1-2) See how great a love the Father has bestowed upon us, that we should be called children of God; and such we are. For this reason the world does not know us, because it did not know Him. 2Beloved, now we are children of God, and it has not appeared as yet what we shall be. We know that, when He appears, we shall be like Him, because we shall see Him just as He is. (1 John 3:1-2).

(John 1:1-5, 11-14, 18, 5:24) In the beginning was the Word, and the Word was with God, and the Word was God. 2He was in the beginning with God. 3All things came into being by Him, and apart from Him nothing came into being that has come into being. 4In Him was life, and the life was the light of men. 5And the light shines in the darkness, and the darkness did not comprehend it.

11He came to His own, and those who were His own did not receive Him. 12But as many as received Him, to them He gave the right to become children of God, even to those who believe in His name, 13who were born not of blood, nor of the will of the flesh, nor of the will of man, but of God. 14 And the Word became flesh, and dwelt among us, and we beheld His glory, glory as of the only begotten from the Father, full of grace and truth.

18No man has seen God at any time; the only begotten God, who is in the bosom of the Father, He has explained Him.

5:24Truly, truly, I say to you, he who hears My words, and believes Him who sent Me, has eternal life, and does not come into judgment, but has passed out of death into life. (John 1:1-5, 11-14, 18, 5:24).

(John 3:17-20) "For God did not send the Son into the world to judge the world, but that the world should be saved through Him. 18" He who believes in Him is not judged; he who does not believe has been judged already, because he has not believed in the name of the only begotten Son of God. 19" And this is the judgment, that the light is come into the world, and men loved the darkness rather than the light; for their deeds were evil. 20" For everyone who does evil hates the light, and does not come to the light, lest his deeds should be exposed. (John 3:17-20).

(Genesis 5:1-3) This is the book of the generations of Adam. In the day when God created man, He made him in the likeness of God. 2He created them male and female, and He blessed them and named them Man in the day when they were created. 3When Adam had lived one hundred and thirty years, he became the father of a son in his own likeness, according to his image, and named him Seth. (Genesis 5:1-3).

(1 John 3:11-12) For this is the message which you have heard from the beginning, that we should love one another; 12not as Cain, who was of the evil one, and slew his brother. And for what reason did he slay him? Because his deeds were evil, and his brother's were righteous. (1 John 3:11-12).

(Ephesians 2:1-3) And you were dead in your trespasses and sins, 2in which you formerly walked according to the course of this world, according to the prince of the power of the air, of the spirit that is now working in the sons of disobedience. 3Among them we too all formerly lived in the lusts of our flesh, indulging the desires of the flesh and of the mind, and were by nature children of wrath, even as the rest. (Ephesians 2:1-3).

(Psalm 51:5) Behold, I was brought forth in iniquity, And in sin my mother conceived me. (Psalm 51:5).

(Judges 2:6-15) When Joshua had dismissed the people, the sons of Israel went each to his inheritance to possess the land. 7And the people served the LORD all the days of Joshua, and all the days of the elders who survived Joshua, who had seen all the great work of the LORD which He had done for Israel. 8Then Joshua the son of Nun, the servant of the LORD, died at the age of one hundred and ten. 9And they buried him in the territory of his inheritance in Timnath-heres, in the hill country of Ephraim, north of Mount Gaash. 10And all that generation also were gathered to their fathers; and there arose another generation after them who did not know the LORD, nor yet the work which He had done for Israel. 11 Then the sons of Israel did evil in the sight of the LORD, and served the Baals, 12and they forsook the LORD, the God of their fathers, who had brought them out of the land of Egypt, and followed other gods from among the gods of the peoples who were around them, and bowed themselves down to them; thus they provoked the LORD to anger. 13So they forsook the LORD and served Baal and the Ashtaroth. 14And the anger of the LORD burned against Israel, and He gave them into the hands of plunderers who plundered them; and He sold them into the hands of their enemies around them, so that they could no longer stand before their enemies. 15Wherever they went, the hand of the LORD was against them for evil, as the LORD had spoken and as the LORD had sworn to them, so that they were severely distressed. (Judges 2:6-15).

(John 8:37-47) "I know that you are Abraham's offspring; yet you seek to kill Me, because My word has no place in you. 38" I speak the things which I have seen with My Father; therefore you also do the things which you heard from your father." 39They answered and said to Him, "Abraham is our father." Jesus said to them, "If you are Abraham's children, do the deeds of Abraham. 40" But as it is, you are seeking to kill Me, a man who has told you the truth, which I heard from God; this Abraham did not do. 41" You are doing the deeds of your father." They said to Him, "We were not born of fornication; we have one Father, even God." 42Jesus said to them, "If God were your Father, you would love

Me; for I proceeded forth and have come from God, for I have not even come on My own initiative, but He sent Me. 43" Why do you not understand what I am saying? It is because you cannot hear My word. 44" You are of your father the devil, and you want to do the desires of your father. He was a murderer from the beginning, and does not stand in the truth, because there is no truth in him. Whenever he speaks a lie, he speaks from his own nature; for he is a liar, and the father of flies. 45" But because I speak the truth, you do not believe Me. 46" Which one of you convicts Me of sin? If I speak truth, why do you not believe Me? 47" He who is of God hears the words of God; for this reason you do not hear them, because you are not of God." (John 8:37-47).

(Romans 3:9-18) What then? Are we better than they? Not at all; for we have already charged that both Jews and Greeks are all under sin; 10as it is written, "THERE IS NONE RIGHTEOUS, NOT EVEN ONE; 11THERE IS NONE WHO UNDERSTANDS, THERE IS NONE WHO SEEKS FOR GOD; 12ALL HAVE TURNED ASIDE, TOGETHER THEY HAVE BECOME USELESS; THERE IS NONE WHO DOES GOOD, THERE IS NOT EVEN ONE." 13" THEIR THROAT IS AN OPEN GRAVE, WITH THEIR TONGUES THEY KEEP DECEIVING," "THE POISON OF ASPS IS UNDER THEIR LIPS"; 14" WHOSE MOUTH IS FULL OF CURSING AND BITTERNESS"; 15" THEIR FEET ARE SWIFT TO SHED BLOOD, 16DESTRUCTION AND MISERY ARE IN THEIR PATHS, 17AND THE PATH OF PEACE HAVE THEY NOT KNOWN." 18" THERE IS NO FEAR OF GOD BEFORE THEIR EYES." (Romans 3:9-18).

(Ephesians 4:17-24) This I say therefore, and affirm together with the Lord, that you walk no longer just as the Gentiles also walk, in the futility of their mind, 18being darkened in their understanding, excluded from the life of God, because of the ignorance that is in them, because of the hardness of their heart; 19and they, having become callous, have given themselves over to sensuality, for the practice of every kind of impurity with greediness. 20But you did not learn Christ in this way, 21if indeed you have heard Him and have been taught in Him, just as truth is in Jesus, 22that, in reference to your former manner of life, you lay aside the old self, which is being corrupted in accordance with the lusts of deceit, 23and that you be renewed in the spirit of your mind, 24and put on the new self, which in the likeness of God has been created in righteousness and holiness of the truth. (Ephesians 4:17-24).

(Romans 5:12-19) Therefore, just as through one man sin entered into the world, and death through sin, and so death spread to all men, because all sinned— 13for until the Law sin was in the world; but sin is not imputed when there is no law. 14Nevertheless death reigned from Adam until Moses, even over those who had not sinned in the likeness of the offense of Adam, who is a type of Him who was to come. 15But the free gift is not like the transgression. For if by the transgression of the one the many died, much more did the grace of God and the gift by the grace of the one Man, Jesus Christ, abound to the many. 16And the gift is not like that which came through the one who sinned; for on the one hand the judgment arose from one transgression resulting in condemnation, but on the other hand the free gift arose from many transgressions resulting in justification. 17For if by the transgression of the one, death reigned through the one, much more those who receive the abundance of grace and of the gift of righteousness will reign in life through the One, Jesus Christ. 18So then as through one transgression there resulted condemnation to all men, even so through one act of righteousness there resulted justification of life to all men. 19For as through the one man's disobedience the many were made sinners, even so through the obedience of the One the many will be made righteous. (Romans 5:12-19).

(1 Thessalonians 4:13-17) But we do not want you to be uninformed, brethren, about those who are asleep, that you may not grieve, as do the rest who have no hope. 14For if we believe that Jesus died and rose again, even so God will bring with Him those who have fallen asleep in Jesus. 15For this we say to you by the word of the Lord, that we who are alive, and remain until the coming of the Lord, shall not precede those who have fallen asleep. 16For the Lord Himself will descend from heaven with a shout, with the voice of the archangel, and with the trumpet of God; and the dead in Christ shall rise first. 17Then we who are alive and remain shall be caught up together with them in the clouds to meet the Lord in the air, and thus we shall always be with the Lord. 18Therefore comfort one another with these words. (1 Thessalonians 4:13-17).

(Matthew 25:31-46) The Judgment: "But when the Son of Man comes in His glory, and all the angels with Him, then He will sit on His glorious throne. 32" And all the nations will be gathered before Him; and He will separate them from one another, as the shepherd separates the sheep from the goats; 33and He will put the sheep on His right, and the goats on the left. 34" Then the King will say to those on His right, 'Come, you who are blessed of My Father, inherit the kingdom prepared for you from the foundation of the world. 35' For I was hungry, and you gave Me something to eat; I was thirsty, and you gave Me drink; I was a stranger, and you invited Me in; 36naked, and you clothed Me; I was sick, and you visited Me; I was in prison, and you came to Me.' 37" Then the righteous will answer Him, saying, 'Lord, when did we see You hungry, and feed You, or thirsty, and give You drink? 38' And when did we see You a stranger, and invite You in, or naked, and clothe You? 39' And when did we see You sick, or in prison, and come to You?' 40" And the King will answer and say to them, 'Truly I say to you, to the extent that you did it to one of these brothers of Mine, even the least of them, you did it to Me.' 41" Then He will also say to those on His left, 'Depart from Me, accursed ones, into the eternal fire which has been prepared for the devil and his angels; 42for I was hungry, and you gave Me nothing to eat; I was thirsty, and you gave Me nothing to drink; 43I was a stranger, and you did not invite Me in; naked, and you did not clothe Me; sick, and in prison, and you did not visit Me.' 44" Then they themselves also will answer, saying, 'Lord, when did we see You hungry, or thirsty, or a stranger, or naked, or sick, or in prison, and did not take care of You?' 45" Then He will answer them, saying, 'Truly I say to you, to the extent that you did not do it to one of the least of these, you did not do it to Me.' 46" And these will go away into eternal punishment, but the righteous into eternal life." (Matthew 25:31-46).

(Revelation 20:1-15) Satan Bound: And I saw an angel coming down from heaven, having the key of the abyss and a great chain in his hand. 2And he laid hold of the dragon, the serpent of old, who is the devil and Satan, and bound him for a thousand years, 3and threw him into the abyss, and shut it and sealed it over him, so that he should not deceive the nations any longer, until the thousand years were completed; after these things he must be released for a short time. 4 And I saw thrones, and they sat upon them, and judgment was given to them. And I saw the souls of those who had been beheaded because of the testimony of Jesus and because of the word of God, and those who had not worshiped the beast or his image, and had not received the mark upon their forehead and upon their hand; and they came to life and reigned with Christ for a thousand years. 5The rest of the dead did not come to life until the thousand years were completed. This is the first resurrection. 6Blessed and holy is the one who has a part in the first resurrection; over these the second death has no power, but they will be priests of God and of Christ and will reign with Him for a thousand years. [Satan Freed, Doomed] 7 And when the thousand years are completed, Satan will be released from his prison, 8and will come out to deceive the nations which are in the four corners of the earth, Gog and Magog, to gather them together for the war; the number of them is like the sand of the seashore. 9And they came up on the broad plain of the earth and surrounded the camp of the saints and the beloved city, and fire came down from heaven and devoured them. 10And the devil who deceived them was thrown into the lake of fire and brimstone, where the beast and the false prophet are also; and they will be tormented day and night forever and ever. [Judgment at the Throne of God] 11 And I saw a great white throne and Him who sat upon it, from whose presence earth and heaven fled away, and no place was found for them. 12And I saw the dead, the great and the small, standing before the throne, and books were opened; and another book was opened, which is the book of life; and the dead were judged from the things which were written in the books, according to their deeds. 13And the sea gave up the dead which were in it, and death and Hades gave up the dead which were in them; and they were judged, every one of them according to their deeds. 14And death and Hades were thrown into the lake of fire. This is the second death, the lake of fire. 15And if anyone's name was not found written in the book of life, he was thrown into the lake of fire. (Revelation 20:1-15).

(1 John 2:2) and He Himself is the propitiation for our sins; and not for ours only, but also for those of the whole world. (1 John 2:2).

(Romans 3:9-12) What then? Are we better than they? Not at all; for we have already charged that both Jews and Greeks are all under sin; 10as it is written, "THERE IS NONE RIGHTEOUS, NOT EVEN ONE; 11THERE IS NONE WHO UNDERSTANDS, THERE IS NONE WHO SEEKS FOR GOD; 12ALL HAVE TURNED ASIDE, TOGETHER THEY HAVE BECOME USELESS; THERE IS NONE WHO DOES GOOD, THERE IS NOT EVEN ONE." (Romans 3:9-12).

(Romans 8:29) For whom He foreknew, He also predestined to become conformed to the image of His Son, that He might be the first-born among many brethren; (Romans 8:29).

(John 3:18) "He who believes in Him is not judged; he who does not believe has been judged already, because he has not believed in the name of the only begotten Son of God. (John

3:18).

(Romans 1:18-32) For the wrath of God is revealed from heaven against all ungodliness and unrighteousness of men, who suppress the truth in unrighteousness, 19because that which is known about God is evident within them; for God made it evident to them. 20For since the creation of the world His invisible attributes, His eternal power and divine nature, have been clearly seen, being understood through what has been made, so that they are without excuse. 21For even though they knew God, they did not honor Him as God, or give thanks; but they became futile in their speculations, and their foolish heart was darkened. 22Professing to be wise, they became fools, 23and exchanged the glory of the incorruptible God for an image in the form of corruptible man and of birds and four-footed animals and crawling creatures. 24 Therefore God gave them over in the lusts of their hearts to impurity, that their bodies might be dishonored among them. 25For they exchanged the truth of God for a lie, and worshiped and served the creature rather than the Creator, who is blessed forever. Amen. 26 For this reason God gave them over to degrading passions; for their women exchanged the natural function for that which is unnatural, 27and in the same way also the men abandoned the natural function of the woman and burned in their desire toward one another, men with men committing indecent acts and receiving in their own persons the due penalty of their error. 28 And just as they did not see fit to acknowledge God any longer, God gave them over to a depraved mind, to do those things which are not proper, 29being filled with all unrighteousness, wickedness, greed, evil; full of envy, murder, strife, deceit, malice; they are gossips, 30slanderers, haters of God, insolent, arrogant, boastful, inventors of evil, disobedient to parents, 31without understanding, untrustworthy, unloving, unmerciful; 32and, although they know the ordinance of God, that those who practice such things are worthy of death, they not only do the same, but also give hearty approval to those who practice them. (Romans 1:18-32).

(John 1:34) "And I have seen, and have borne witness that this is the Son of God." (John 1:34).

(2 Corinthians 5:17) Therefore if any man is in Christ, he is a new creature; the old things passed away; behold, new things have come. (2 Corinthians 5:17).

(Colossians 1:15) And He is the image of the invisible God, the first born of all creation. (Colossians 1:15).

(Ephesians 4:11-13) And He gave some as apostles, and some as prophets, and some as evangelists, and some as pastors and teachers, 12for the equipping of the saints for the work of service, to the building up of the body of Christ; 13until we all attain to the unity of the faith, and of the knowledge of the Son of God, to a mature man, to the measure of the stature which belongs to the fullness of Christ. (Ephesians 4:11-13).

(Galatians 5:16-26) But I say, walk by the Spirit, and you will not carry out the desire of the flesh. 17For the flesh sets its desire against the Spirit, and the Spirit against the flesh; for these are in opposition to one another, so that you may not do the things that you please. 18But if you are led by the Spirit, you are not under the Law. 19Now the deeds of the flesh are evident, which are: immorality, impurity, sensuality, 20idolatry, sorcery, enmities, strife, jealousy, outbursts of anger, disputes, dissensions, factions, 21envying, drunkenness, carousing, and things like these, of which I forewarn you just as I have forewarned you that those who practice such things shall not inherit the kingdom of God. 22But the fruit of the Spirit is love, joy, peace, patience, kindness, goodness, faithfulness, 23gentleness, self-control; against such things there is no law. 24Now those who belong to Christ Jesus have crucified the flesh with its passions and desires. 25 If we live by the Spirit, let us also walk by the Spirit. 26Let us not become boastful, challenging one another, envying one another. (Galatians 5:16-26).

(Romans 7:14-25) For we know that the Law is spiritual; but I am of flesh, sold into bondage to sin. 15For that which I am doing, I do not understand; for I am not practicing what I would like to do, but I am doing the very thing I hate. 16But if I do the very thing I do not wish to do, I agree with the Law, confessing that it is good. 17So now, no longer am I the one doing it, but sin which dwells me. 18For I know that nothing good dwells in me, that is, in my flesh; for the wishing is present in me, but the doing of the good is not. 19For the good that I wish, I do not do; but I practice the very evil that I do not wish. 20But if I am doing the very thing I do not wish, I am no longer the one doing it, but sin which dwells in me. 21I find then the principle that evil is present in me, the one who wishes to do good. 22For I joyfully concur with the law of God in the inner man, 23but I see a different law in the members of my body, waging war against the law of my mind, and making me a prisoner of the law of sin which is in my members. 24Wretched man that I am! Who will set me free from the body of this death? 25Thanks be to God through Jesus Christ our Lord! So then, on the one hand I myself with my mind am serving the law of God, but on the other, with my flesh the law of sin. (Romans 7:14-25).

(Philippians 2:3-16) Do nothing from selfishness or empty conceit, but with humility of mind let each of you regard one another as more important than himself; 4do not merely look out for your own personal interests, but also for the interests of others. 5Have this attitude in yourselves which was also in Christ Jesus, 6who, although He existed in the form of God, did not regard equality with God a thing to be grasped, 7but emptied Himself, taking the form of a bond-servant, and being made in the likeness of men. 8And being found in appearance as a man, He humbled Himself by becoming obedient to the point of death, even death on a cross. 9Therefore also God highly exalted Him, and bestowed on Him the name which is above every name, 10that at the name of Jesus EVERY KNEE SHOULD BOW, of those who are in heaven, and on earth, and under the earth, 11and that every tongue should confess that Jesus Christ is Lord, to the glory of God the Father. 12 So then, my beloved, just as you have always obeyed, not as in my presence only, but now much more in my absence, work out your salvation with fear and trembling; 13for it is God who is at work in you, both to will and to work for His good pleasure. 14Do all things without grumbling or disputing; 15that you may prove yourselves to be blameless and innocent, children of God above reproach in the midst of a crooked and perverse generation, among whom you appear as lights (Philippians 2:3-16).

(Romans 12:3) For through the grace given to me I say to

every man among you not to think more highly of himself than he ought to think; but to think so as to have sound judgment, as God has allotted to each a measure of faith. (Romans 12:3).

(Isaiah 14:12-15) "How you have fallen from heaven, O star of the morning, son of the dawn! You have been cut down to the earth, You who have weakened the nations! 13" But you said in your heart, 'I will ascend to heaven; I will raise my throne above the stars of God, And I will sit on the mount of assembly In the recesses of the north. 14' I will ascend above the heights of the clouds; I will make myself like the Most High.' 15" Nevertheless you will be thrust down to Sheol, To the recesses of the pit. (Isaiah 14:12-15).

(Galatians 3:26-29) For you are all sons of God through faith in Christ Jesus. 27For all of you who were baptized into Christ have clothed yourselves with Christ. 28There is neither Jew nor Greek, there is neither slave nor free man, there is neither male nor female; for you are all one in Christ Jesus. 29And if you belong to Christ, then you are Abraham's offspring, heirs according to promise. (Galatians 3:26-29).

(Hebrews 12:4-11) You have not yet resisted to the point of shedding blood in your striving against sin; 5and you have forgotten the exhortation which is addressed to you as sons, "MY SON, DO NOT REGARD LIGHTLY THE DISCIPLINE OF THE LORD, NOR FAINT WHEN YOU ARE REPROVED BY HIM; 6FOR THOSE WHOM THE LORD LOVES HE DISCIPLINES, AND HE SCOURGES EVERY SON WHOM HE RECEIVES." 7It is for discipline that you endure; God deals with you as with sons; for what son is there whom his father does not discipline? 8But if you are without discipline, of which all have become partakers, then you are illegitimate children and not sons. 9Furthermore, we had earthly fathers to discipline us, and we respected them; shall we not much rather be subject to the Father of spirits, and live? 10For they disciplined us for a short time as seemed best to them, but He disciplines us for our good, that we may share His holiness. 11All discipline for the moment seems not to be joyful, but sorrowful; yet to those who have been trained by it, afterwards it yields the peaceful fruit of righteousness. (Hebrews 12:4-11).

(Hebrews 12:18-29) For you have not come to a mountain that may be touched and to a blazing fire, and to darkness and gloom and whirlwind, 19and to the blast of a trumpet and the sound of words which sound was such that those who heard begged that no further word should be spoken to them. 20For they could not bear the command, "IF EVEN A BEAST TOUCHES THE MOUNTAIN, IT WILL BE STONED." 21And so terrible was the sight, that Moses said, "I AM FULL OF FEAR and trembling." 22But you have come to Mount Zion and to the city of the living God, the heavenly Jerusalem, and to myriads of angels, 23to the general assembly and church of the first-born who are enrolled in heaven, and to God, the Judge of all, and to the spirits of righteous men made perfect, 24and to Jesus, the mediator of a new covenant, and to the sprinkled blood, which speaks better than the blood of Abel. 25See to it that you do not refuse Him who is speaking. For if those did not escape when they refused him who warned them on earth, much less shall we escape who turn away from Him who warns from heaven. 26And His voice shook the earth then, but now He has promised, saying,

"YET ONCE MORE I WILL SHAKE NOT ONLY THE EARTH, BUT ALSO THE HEAVEN." 27And this expression, "Yet once more," denotes the removing of those things which can be shaken, as of created things, in order that those things which cannot be shaken may remain. 28Therefore, since we receive a kingdom which cannot be shaken, let us show gratitude, by which we may offer to God an acceptable service with reverence and awe; 29for our God is a consuming fire. (Hebrews 12:18-29).

(John 14:21-24) "He who has My commandments and keeps them, he it is who loves Me; and he who loves Me shall be loved by My Father, and I will love him, and will disclose Myself to him." 22Judas (not Iscariot) *said to Him, "Lord, what then has happened that You are going to disclose Yourself to us, and not to the world?" 23Jesus answered and said to him, "If anyone loves Me, he will keep My word; and My Father will love him, and We will come to him, and make Our abode with him. 24" He who does not love Me does not keep My words; and the word which you hear is not Mine, but the Father's who sent Me. (John 14:21-24).

(Luke 9:23-24) And He was saying to them all, "If anyone wishes to come after Me, let him deny himself, and take up his cross daily, and follow Me. 24" For whoever wishes to save his life shall lose it, but whoever loses his life for My sake, he is the one who will save it. (Luke 9:23-24).

(Deuteronomy 6:4-9) "Hear, O Israel! The LORD [Yahweh] is our God, the LORD [Yahweh] is one! 5"And you shall love the LORD [Yahweh] your God with all your heart and with all your soul and with all your might. 6"And these words, which I am commanding you today, shall be on your heart; 7and you shall teach them *diligently* to your sons and shall talk of them when you sit in your house and when you walk by the way and when you lie down and when you rise up. 8"And you shall bind them as a sign on your hand and they shall be as frontals on your forehead. 9"And you shall write them on the doorposts of your house and on your gates. (Deuteronomy 6:4-9). [Brackets and italics mine].